THE PROSPERITY PRINCIPLES
BY
TANYA MARCHIOL

The Prosperity Principles

The Prosperity Principles

Tanya Marchiol
Copyright ©2013

Printed in the United States of America
Cover design: Select-O-Grafix, LLC
Text Layout: Select-O-Grafix, LLC
ISBN: 978-0-9890127-0-6

The Prosperity Principles

DEDICATION

This book is dedicated to the most important and influential people in my life...my mom and dad. For all the years you believed in me, never let me quit, and carried me through life's rough spots, I could never say thank you enough. Life is a continual battle but my upbringing based on Jesus Christ, and having parents like you made it easier. You were not afraid to discipline me, tell me no, or lift me up when needed. There are no words to express my gratitude for the person you've molded me to be. The positive affirmations and the "never quit" attitude prevail today. I talk to you both every morning and every evening and you are my best friends. I love you!

ACKNOWLEDGMENTS

Mom, Dad, Grandpa Joe, Dr. Julie Marchiol, and Ken Marchiol. Mr. John Letellier, Dr. Mary Gill, Shannon Sharpe, Stuart Varney, Jake Novak, Kelly McKenna, Tanya Player, Eddie Rhodam, Mark Goldmann, Ryan McCormick, Kathleen Birmingham, and of course the ones I come home to daily, Flakes, Lexus, Azure, Dolce, Vita, and the best friend I've ever had, Capo!

CONTENTS

FOREWORD

Tanya Marchiol's business, Team Investments, would have been nothing but a pipe dream without the positive attitude and hard work ethic she was raised with. Both of these helped Tanya to believe that she can do anything she puts her mind to.

Everything is possible.

Having worked with many of today's successful entrepreneurs, I recognize the traits of just such a rising star. It isn't easy to find good role models such as Tanya and her business, Team Investments.

Why?

Blame it on the overabundance of self-help books, gurus, and experts. Many inspirational speakers had a lucky break and learned how to capitalize on it. Tanya, however, has lived a life where she learned exactly how to be successful. Then, when a freak accident turned her life upside down, all the lessons she had been studying, learning, and incorporating into her life came to her aid. She overcame major challenges in order to be where she is today. It would have been all too easy for her to sit back and say, "I just didn't get the right break in life."

Without those lessons, Tanya's words in this book would fall flat and this would be just another "flash in the pan" inspirational book. Tanya's wisdom, understanding, and appreciation for what it means to be looking for prosperity sets her apart from those who claim to understand, but have never struggled. Metal that has been tempered or tested by fire and hammer is stronger than untested metal.

We have all met people who have big plans, and grandiose ideas. And when they're talking, we see the picture they paint. It is exciting. We want to be part of their dream. Then, the next time we meet them, they are on to the next idea without ever doing anything about their first idea. What happened? They had a good idea, but there was no follow through.

Tanya grew up understanding that your word was your bond. At the age of seven she wanted to play softball. Her parents gave her permission to play, but cautioned that once she joined the team, there would be no quitting. Tanya's first time at bat was a disaster. She stood on the wrong side of the plate. She had the bat over the wrong shoulder. Anything that could have gone wrong for her that first game did go wrong. At home she wanted to quit. She sobbed. She begged. She pleaded to be allowed to quit this sport that she now hated. Fortunately for Tanya, her parents insisted on her keeping her word. She wanted to play Little League; they insisted she play until the end of the season, despite the challenges. Baseball is still not her favorite sport to play, but she today she can hold her head up high and say, "I finished the season. I kept my word."

That lesson taught Tanya to keep her word to herself, and that is what is found in her first book, *The Prosperity Principles*. By learning to keep your word to yourself, anything and everything is possible. Here you will find objective and practical advice to help you become the prosperous person you have always known you can be.

Put to practice the lessons contained here and a more prosperous life is within your grasp. Maintaining a positive attitude, working hard, and keeping your word to yourself will change your life. Who knows, maybe you will become a role model for someone else just as Tanya has become a role model for thousands of people.

Kathleen Birmingham
Phoenix, Arizona
March 17, 2013

INTRODUCTION

My siblings and I were raised to believe that with a positive attitude and hard work we could succeed at anything. I've applied that mentality to every aspect of my life beginning with athletic achievement and later building a profitable business. The "everything is possible" philosophy forms the backbone of *The Prosperity Principles.*

My parents raised my brother, sister, and me in a positive, supportive environment. Negativity was not an option. Every day my mother would tell us we could do anything we set our minds to.

We had our mouths washed out with soap if we used the word "can't."

Our parents expected us to succeed, and succeed we did. We each received full scholarships and graduated from universities. My brother and I earned athletic scholarships while my sister received an academic scholarship to Princeton. Each of us had the "everything is possible" mentality ingrained in our brains and we used it in our own individual ways.

While I never considered anything to be beyond my reach, as a young girl I did not expect to succeed in the financial world. My initial accomplishments were in the athletic arena.

In high school, I used the "everything is possible" mantra as a motivating force to succeed on the volleyball court. I was dedicated and enthusiastic. I pushed myself and focused on being the best volleyball player I could be. The more I succeeded, the harder I worked and the greater the "everything is possible" message grew in intensity.

Each of us, whether we are prosperous already or not, should run our lives with prosperity in mind. It is my belief that over time we grow more afraid to reach for our full financial potential and more convinced it is an unattainable goal.

Those perceptions are wrong. Anyone can achieve financial prosperity and lasting wealth by using my five basic principles.

As you continue reading, I'll share with you my Prosperity Principles, how I developed them and share with you ways you can incorporate them into your life.

PRINCIPLE 1: MAKE WISE DECISIONS
PRINCIPLE 2: LEAD YOUR WEALTH
PRINCIPLE 3: RUN YOUR LIFE LIKE A BUSINESS
PRINCIPLE 4: ALWAYS CREATE CASH FLOW
PRINCIPLE 5: MONEY DOES GROW ON TREES

I developed these principles as a result of the curve-balls life threw at me. I found myself in a great deal of debt, and using these principles I not only managed to pay off my debt, but I created a multimillion-dollar business, and, most importantly, reshaped my financial future. I continue to use these principles to expand upon all I have accumulated, continuing to build generational wealth for my future family.

Using these principles now, you can avoid the anxiety that comes with losing a job or breaking an ankle. Relying on our money to work for us is necessary to achieve financial freedom. There are a thousand valid reasons to work; enjoyment, contribution to society, health, human interaction, and gratification are just a few, but working solely because we need that paycheck is disheartening. There are better ways to make money without working every day for the rest of our lives.

Before you read on, pause for a second and remember yourself as you were as a child; your mind was wide open to anything and everything.

While your dreams were massive and unhindered, your parents probably told you anything is possible with hard work. They told you that knowledge is power.

They were right.
With dedication and education, anything is possible.

The Prosperity Principles

LIFE HAPPENS

A flash of blue sky, a close-up of well-manicured green grass, then in one split second, and my life changed permanently.

One minute I was buzzing along in a golf cart, enjoying the glorious Arizona sunshine. The next, I was struggling to keep the cart from tipping over and reflexively, I put my left foot out to steady myself, but physics and gravity were more powerful than I. We tumbled to the ground, the cart and I, and when the world stopped moving, I was trapped underneath the golf cart, unable to free myself.

At first I thought, "I'll just push it off of me."

It wasn't that easy.

Never before had I been so trapped. Any jam I found myself in, I would get myself out. All my life I had learned to be self-sufficient, to be strong, and to take care of things by myself. One more time, I pushed at the mass of metal and leather, but the cart didn't budge.

Oh my God! I need help. How do I do this? How do I call for help? I weakly called out, "Help, I'm trapped."

Pathetic.

And it got no attention.

Finally, I screamed for help, and a couple guys dropped their golf clubs and jogged over to my rescue. They moved the cart off of me, but then cautioned me to sit still while they called an ambulance. I thought they were over-reacting, but did as they suggested.

Using my cell phone, I dialed my mom's number. I just wanted someone to know I'd been hurt. Shock must have slowed my responses because I wasn't feeling very much pain yet. I told my mom I thought I may have broken a bone and that I might need stitches so I would be going to the hospital. By this time, the paramedics were there. They let me finish my call, and then they said, "You're not just going to the hospital; you're going in for emergency surgery."

My brain didn't register the words "emergency surgery," I was sure I had only broken a bone. They rushed me to Phoenix General, where the best foot surgeon was, telling me, "Tanya, you're about to lose your foot. You have to be seen immediately."

Were these guys crazy?

I wasn't that hurt!

When I got to the hospital, they rushed me in and began to clean up my leg. The pain medication they gave me didn't quite dull the pain, and I felt absolutely everything they were doing as they worked on my leg. The pain-dulling effect of shock had worn off. From my knee to the top of my toes my skin was shredded and looked like hamburger meat.

The accident severed all the tendons to my toes and had torn off so much of my flesh there was not enough blood pumping from my leg to my foot. They would have to do skin grafts, and then recreate blood vessels to save my foot.

For the next six months I was hospitalized and went through thirteen surgeries to rebuild my foot. The doctor asked me if I wanted the skin graft to come from my butt or my stomach. I was an athlete, and felt I had a pretty perfect butt, so I asked him take the graft from my stomach.

For a long time afterward, I fixated on the scar on my stomach that stretched from hip bone to hip bone.

Up until that point in my life, I had been a professional athlete. I'd played volleyball all the way through high school and in college, completing two years as a professional player in Italy. Until the accident, I had been working at the golf course because it was a physical job, the kind an athlete desires.

Learning to walk again was a trip.

My doctor told me that I would probably never run again, and I would be lucky if I walked right. My entire world had been destroyed in the blink of an eye. Before this, my life's greatest accomplishment had been volleyball. I'd had a perfect body. I had never been hurt. I had been an athlete my whole life.

Now, I couldn't even walk.

My parents took turns coming to Phoenix to be with me. One week it was my mom, the next week it was my dad. I had tons of friends who visited me during my recovery, and the floor nurses knew that there was almost always a party in my room. But, the whole time I was laughing with my friends I was trying to ignore a voice deep down inside me that just wouldn't be silenced. It kept saying over and over, "You're nothing."

Eventually, I listened to that voice and I had some really low times in the hospital. My entire life my whole image had been caught up in being the best athlete I could be. It was all about looks and being the best, physically, at my sport. There was zero substance. I had never developed anything of substance about myself because I'd spent all my time being the best athlete.

Now, I had a messed up leg. I had a scar on my arm. I had a scar on my abdomen. While I was in the hospital, I really did fight. It's the way I'm made. It's "fight or flight," and I always chose "fight." But once I was released, I had a big problem.

What's next?

And this is what all athletes go through. People don't care if you're nice or mean, smart or stupid. They care if you're a good athlete.

Now I was ugly.

I wasn't just scarred. I was marred.

I had no identity. No character. I was no longer perfect. I could never play volleyball again.

What was I going to do?

While I was in the hospital, my mom had bought me some books on real estate and I read them just for something to do. Once I got out of the hospital, I decided I had to do something, so I went ahead and took the required real estate classes to get my license, but it was not my passion. I went back to the golf course, working in the snack shack just to put a little bit of money in my pocket, but it was barely enough to live on, much less pay the mountains of medical bills I'd managed to accumulate over the previous six months. I'm not even sure how I made my mortgage payments during that time.

I probably could have floated along in self-pity and misery for a very long time, feeling sorry for myself, wondering what I could possibly do with my life. Everyone who would listen heard my tale of woe over and over again. One day, I was sitting with a friend in her bathroom. I was crying. Yes, I was wallowing in self-pity and showing her the scar on my stomach. My leg didn't bother me; I knew it was going to be OK.

It was the scar on my stomach that I just couldn't let go of.

The door to the bathroom opened with such force that it banged against the wall. My friend's husband had heard enough. "Tanya, if you think that no one will ever love you because you have a scar on your stomach, then you're totally crazy!" Then he slammed the door and stormed down the hallway.

He'd obviously heard enough of me complaining.

That was my defining moment.

As quickly as my accident occurred, I realized that I had to change everything I thought about myself. I knew I was so much more than the scar, so much more than my body.

I had no choice but to figure out my life.

And this is where the lessons I'd learned all my life came into play.

*****

Growing up, everything my parents did was a struggle, but I never knew it. My dad was the athletic coach for a small high school and my mom worked two jobs, one for the State of Colorado, and the other as a waitress. While my parents couldn't provide a lot materially as we were growing up, they made sure my brother, my sister, and I knew what perseverance was.

Being a football coach, my dad would often take my older brother and me to the school where he had us race on the football field. It didn't matter to my dad that my brother was a boy and nine years older than I was. He made us race over and over until I could finally beat my brother, eventually my brother would let me win.

He taught me to never, *never, **never*** quit.

I remember playing baseball for Little League. High Country Fly was our team. I remember I was not a baseball player. The first time I committed to it, but I hated every minute of it. I wanted to play baseball that summer, my team sucked, and my mother would not let me quit. The first time I was up to bat, (I am right handed) I stood up there with the bat over my left shoulder.

Everyone laughed and was yelling at me to turn around.

I was mortified.

I didn't know what I was going to do. I struck out. I don't think I ever hit a ball that season. But, my mom wouldn't let me quit because that was something I had committed to. I remember, as a kid, my dad always said, "If you're going to do something give one hundred percent or don't do it at all."

There was never a moment in my life where I was allowed to give even just a little bit less than a hundred percent without getting into trouble. While most of my lessons came to me in athletics, it applied everywhere. Saturday was chore day and each of us kids had to take care of our room and one other room in the house. My mom literally used the white-glove test and bounced quarters off our beds to make sure they were made right. My brother trapped me in my room for an hour until I learned how to spell Mississippi. Everything was done to the best of my ability. If we were going to do something, we were going to do it right.

My brother, sister, and I all learned from a very young age you never quit. It was fight or flight, and we learned to fight for everything.

When I was in the fourth grade, my mom got a good job offer, so she and I moved away from my dad and my older sister. My brother was already in college. In deciding where to live in Denver, my mom wanted me to attend school in the wealthiest district possible. We had nothing to our name, but my mom wanted me to have the benefit of knowing how to behave around everyone. She had never had such an advantage, so she continued to work two jobs to get it for me.

The students in my school were driven to school in BMWs and Porsches. They lived in mansions. I lived in a little three bedroom townhouse. I walked to school and because my mom was always working, the lady across the street would watch me until my mom got home. Mom made me learn what it was like to live wealthy, even though we didn't have it.

She put me in classes to learn how to walk, how to talk, where my napkin went, and which spoon or fork to use. My mom wanted me to have this knowledge because she never wanted me to feel inferior by not knowing how to behave in a particular situation.

Looking back, I can really appreciate everything my mom did for me. At the time, I thought I was in hell. I'd been taken out of a situation where everyone knew my dad because he was the athletic director of the high school. As a result, everyone knew me too. But in Denver, I was thrust into a situation where I was with a bunch of kids I didn't have anything in common with.

I cried all the time that first year. I took a three hour bus ride to see my dad every weekend.

By the time I was in the sixth grade, I was enrolled in some self-help classes after school. These weren't just for the students, but for parents too and my mom attended them with me. Every morning we had to say:

You can try and fail, try and fail, try and fail again,
You can try and fail,
But when you fail to try,
You will never win.

That class reinforced everything I had ever learned in my life; you simply *do not* quit anything.

In the seventh grade I discovered volleyball and I loved it. I was always a little athlete, it was what I knew. At one time I wanted to be the first female professional basketball player and I was really good at basketball, but as time went on, I realized I *loved* volleyball.

My mom's second job paid for my club volleyball. I played on the best teams. I had skills. I was really good and it was fun. From that point forward volleyball was my thing. I still played basketball and still ran track all the way through my freshman year in high school, but volleyball was my new passion.

I made the varsity team as a freshman in high school. I was always the one who was in the gym before practice started. I would serve fifty serves to every serving area (there were six when I played). Then, after practice I would serve one hundred serves to every serving area after everyone left. I wore special shoes, jump training shoes that had a platform on the ball and toe of my foot, but they basically had no heel.

I was always on my toes.

I practiced in those shoes and then I would go and run hills in those shoes. There was going to be no one who was going to be better than me on the volleyball court. No one was going to jump higher. No one was going to have a better serve. No one!

It wasn't just the ninety minutes we practiced...I practiced thirty minutes before, then the hour-and-a-half practice, then another hour-and-a-half *after* practice doing things I just made up, like those 600 serves in jump training shoes, or running "suicides" on my own.

I was good at volleyball, and doing all this extra work made me even better.

At the time, I didn't realize that all that extra work would figure into what I became thirty years later. In my sophomore year, Cherry Creek took State, and they had never taken State before. Then in my senior year we took State again.

That was my success story in high school.

*****

When it came time for college recruiting, we didn't have money for someone to make a recruitment tape for me. Most of the really good athletes had VHS tapes created showing them in action playing their sport to be sent to colleges. I had to figure out a way to create a VHS recruiting tape. So, every day after school, I had the AV librarians help me cut my tapes. I made my own recruitment tapes and I sent them out to the various schools I was interested in attending.

I sent my recruiting tapes out to twenty-five schools. I was getting inquiries from a lot of California schools....my vertical jump was about thirty-six inches, which is insane, but it was due to all that working out in the jump shoes.

People came to my mom's house to meet her and she interviewed those coaches, figuring out where I was going to go. A recruiter from Indiana University came up to me and asked if I were Tanya. "Yes," I replied. "Have you seen the tapes of me playing?"

"Well...we got your recruiting tape...it was a great gimmick."

I looked at her, puzzled.

She said, "The whole tape was Winnie-the-Pooh. I thought it was a recruiting ploy, I thought you put this on so we would remember you, but it was all Winnie-the-Pooh. We've heard about you, but have never seen you play." I was mortified, this time for not double checking what I sent out. My sister's favorite cartoon was Winnie the Pooh and I must have grabbed one of her tapes instead. Fortunately for me, they were intrigued by my approach. They watched the game and then came over to the house afterward. They wanted me to visit the school. They knew about my brother, my family. They took the time to find out the facts about me, my family, and my life. It's nice when people take that kind of time to get to know about you and your family.

I signed with Indiana instantly.

Once I got there, the glitz, glam, and show were over.

It was the most intense struggle of my life to that point because while I was good, I wasn't the only one who was good. At the college level *everyone* was good. I wasn't the greatest any more. I had to fight for my position. I'd been trained so long in high school that I knew I could be the best. In college I was put in a position where I wasn't the best anymore and I had to struggle all over again.

Because of that, Indiana was difficult for me, and some of the experiences I had there were horrible. More of my perseverance skills came from college because starting in my sophomore year I hated my coach and yet I still loved volleyball. The coach who recruited me left in my sophomore year and my new coach wasn't a good fit for me.

I'm very intense at what I do. I'm the kind of person where you either love me or you hate me and there is no middle ground. She hated me. I will never forget the I in the Indiana symbol on the court, she sat me down in the middle of the I with her finger in my face, and told me how terrible I was and how I would never go anywhere with volleyball.

That just motivated me.

I remember thinking, "Do you know who you're talking to?" It seemed there was nothing I could do right in her eyes. I was a top player. I was liked. I was producing. But when it came to my coach, it was oil and water.

During my junior year in college my grandfather died. He was that grandparent you just adored. It was 2:23 AM. I couldn't sleep. I went out into the hallway (we had to stay in the dorm during pre-season). Something prompted me to call my mom and ask about my brother and sister and then I asked about my grandpa. She didn't want to tell me because it was my dad's dad, even though she knew he had passed away just a minute or two before I had called. Somehow I had known.

The next day I was pulled out of practice to answer a phone call from my dad, telling me about my grandfather's death. I went home for the funeral and missed a week of practice and games. During that time, I don't know if my coach thought that I wasn't serious any more or what happened, but when I came back our relationship was even worse. We just couldn't stand each other. It got so bad that during my senior year my coach tried to get me kicked off the team for breaking curfew.

It was battle after battle after battle. The first half of my senior year was awful.

Mid-way through my senior year I chose to finish classes in Florence, Italy, and play volleyball while I was there. I loved being there, but I didn't love the volleyball there. The passion and desire I had for volleyball was gone.

This was the first time I wondered about my future. I had to figure out what I wanted to do. I had no camaraderie, no friends. It was a time in my life I felt really low and alone.

Living in Italy was amazing, but not fulfilling. I came home and I was completely lost, having no idea what I wanted to do. After a six year relationship breakup, not having a job, and not having volleyball, I moved to Arizona on a whim. I had no plan or drive or anything. I got an apartment with a cat, a dog, a pre-paid cell phone, and a blow up mattress. That's it. I became a cart girl on the golf course and I was a trainer at a gym. Soon I was making enough money on the golf course that I quit the gym training.

That's when the cart flipped and landed on my ankle.

The Prosperity Principles

REALITY CHECK

Have you ever received your paycheck for a week or two weeks of work, only to realize that every penny must be spent on the bills that have piled up on your kitchen counter? It's even worse when you realize that the amount of your check barely covers one-third of the bills that are due.

After my accident, I was in this situation and it left me feeling hopeless and frustrated. I paced the floor, wondering what to do next. Should I get another job? Borrow money that I might not be able to pay back? Forget about the bills? The problems seemed so overwhelming that I just ignored them. I would continue to do what I had been doing, living paycheck to paycheck, never managing to move forward. There didn't seem to be a way to break the cycle and it didn't seem as if anything else would work.

This pattern ended when I made a conscious decision to think differently.

You can do this, too.

The creation and achievement of your financial vision isn't hindered by your ability. They are prevented only by your thoughts. I'd been brought up to never allow myself to think negatively. Here was a time when I had to consciously incorporate this belief into my daily thoughts.

Think of it this way. Your current financial situation exists because of your belief system and your thought process. You learned from your parents, your grandparents, a mentor or some other authority figure you admired. But those beliefs and actions put you in a frustrating, dissatisfying place.

Why not make it better?

Start by changing your thought patterns. Once you have developed a new attitude about money and a new mindset, you can begin changing your actions. When you change your actions you will change your financial situation.

I am going to be honest with you: there is no easy way to wealth and abundance. Making money requires proper planning, execution and effort. Often, you will be doing things outside your comfort level.

Remember this as you read the material in this book:

If you continue to do what you've always done, you will continue to get what you have always gotten.

Changing your thoughts about money will change the way you handle money.

Views about Money

There is space at the back of this book for making notes and writing lists. Sometimes I'll ask you to make a list that

I will want you to keep, one that you will need to refer to more than once.

For this first exercise, though, it is better to use loose paper. You'll see why in a few minutes. You will need both a pen and a pencil, too.

What are some of the negative ways you look at money?

Write down each of these thoughts on a piece of paper with a pencil. Write down every single thought that pops into your mind. Be sure to write this list in pencil.

Here are some examples of my negative thoughts about money:

- Money doesn't grow on trees
- Easy come, easy go
- The rich get richer while the poor get poorer
- Money is evil
- It takes money to have money and I don't have any
- Some people are just lucky with money and I am not one of them
- Money can't buy happiness, so why bother to try to make a lot?
- I am self-conscious about my ability to make money; I didn't even go to college, so why should I be able to make a lot of money?
- I am way too busy to think about money
- I wouldn't know where to begin to try to fix my financial problems or to invest money
- The topic of taking charge of my money scares me

- I don't trust the scam artists that might steer me in the wrong direction

I am sure you have plenty of other negative feelings about money.

Most people do.

The important thing is to get those thoughts out of your mind and onto a piece of paper. Allowing these thoughts to clog up your mind slows your path to prosperity. Negative thoughts have never helped anyone achieve their goals.

For the next part of this exercise, take a second piece of paper. This time, I want you to use a pen. Write down the exact opposite of each of your negative statements.

For example, here are the positive statements that counteract my list of negative statements:

- Money is everywhere and easily accessible to me
- Easy come, easy go, easy come again
- The rich get richer and the poor get rich and stay rich
- Money is good
- I do not need money to make money
- With the right kind of hard work, money is possible for everyone
- Money affords financial comfort and a sense of security and it provides whatever luxuries I want
- Formal education and money are not related
- I am never too busy to spend time on my own financial prosperity
- I can start at the beginning just like any other new activity

- Making money is straightforward and easy if I take the time to learn the process myself
- I can learn about making money. The more I know the better I can protect my own interests

Now that you have made your lists, take the page of negative statements and, for each individual statement, think about the specific reasons for your feelings.

For example, if you think "It takes money to make money", it may be because you know someone who has a lot of disposable income. You may see this person as someone who has the ability to invest in money-generating opportunities, someone who seems to make more money with little or no effort, without research and without risk. It becomes natural for you to assume that the only thing preventing you from doing the same thing is a lack of funds. You think, "if only I had the money, I could do that, too."

Now look at the opposite statement, "I do not need money to make money." Begin to play the devil's advocate by fully convincing yourself of the positive statements. Negative statements are just cop-outs and poor excuses that people use to avoid taking control of their lives. Think of some concrete examples you can use to challenge the validity of those negative statements. For instance, when you got your first job, you didn't have money, just the willingness to start working hard and making money. Think about what you have to offer now that could help you make money: connections, materials you own, good credit, services or ideas that someone wants to purchase.

The easiest way to dissolve your negative notions is to think of real examples and real people that will prove that your positive statements are true. When we challenge our own views, we stop seeing everything through a negative prism. Instead, we see workable solutions.

Coming up with examples from your own experience will boost your confidence. If you simply write down positive statements without backing them up, you will have a harder time believing in those statements. The statements will not be motivational and they will not be reassuring. Use someone else's examples if necessary; just make sure you are successfully contradicting every negative statement.

Now, erase everything you wrote down in pencil.

Keep the page with your positive statements handy, because you will want to reread these positive affirmations every single day. Read this list aloud and contemplate what each statement means to you. Remember how my personal development teacher in seventh grade made us repeat that mantra about trying and failing? I learned that over thirty years ago and yet those words course through my mind every day now. That is the power of repeating positive statements on a daily basis. You may want to copy this list onto a page at the back of this book to make sure it is easily accessible and in a safe place.

This exercise is so important because you must recognize how your negative views about money have been preventing your ability to move toward financial stability and then move beyond financial stability into financial abundance.

Once you see your list of negative thoughts written out, and then erased, you can begin to change your behavior. Your positive affirmations about money will serve as a touchstone for you, a place you can return again and again as you build your financial freedom.

Success is your Destiny

Now that you have mastered removing your old thoughts about money and replaced them with positive ideas about money you have passed over one of the most difficult hurdles.

You are now free to create a lifestyle based on financial freedom. That lifestyle is at your fingertips – all that remains is for you to start the work.

A word of caution—don't look back!

Once you have made the decision to pursue the path to prosperity, focus on your destination. If you continue to cling to some of your old beliefs, even in the smallest sense, you might convince yourself that changing your financial situation is a silly idea or a lost cause. Your old beliefs may create a feeling of fear or of doubt. This is why it is so important to immediately discard your old habits and embark on your venture into new territory.

The path to prosperity may sometimes cross difficult terrain. Instead of approaching these difficulties with dread or fear, approach them as if they are a challenge that you are destined to win.

Remember the thoughts about money that you erased?

Those are gone.

They represent the instability and uncertainty that you are now walking away from.

Now look again at your positive affirmations. They are written in ink to signify their permanence. It may be a good idea to keep a copy of these affirmations in more than one place: in your car, in your kitchen, in your office and in the back of this book. That way you will have more opportunities to read them and recite them daily. Whenever you feel doubtful about the path you have chosen, turn to these affirmations to reinforce your drive to success.

Focus on Positivity

Focus on what you want, not on what you don't want.

This is why you must reject your old beliefs about money because they are responsible for putting you where you are right now. Instead of focusing on wanting to get out of debt, not being able to get out of debt, and being tired of your dead end job, shift your focus. Instead, think about creating a continuous flow of money in your life, becoming well-equipped to do achieve it and becoming a person who leads his entire life like a business. You can start by reciting out loud the positive statements on your list.

You may feel foolish repeating statements out loud. If you do, think about that quote I mentioned earlier: "If you continue to do what you've always done, you will continue to get what you have always gotten." If you want to move forward, you are going to have to do some things that you are not accustomed to doing. Doing this may seem silly or pointless, but it has been proven that when you verbalize your beliefs those very beliefs become reality. Thoughts become words, words become actions, actions create character and character is what others see in us.

> **Thoughts ->Words ->Actions -> Character**

If you want change, you must create an environment in which change can flourish.

Know your Destination

I love to use the example of getting directions. How do you get directions from someone if you don't know where you are? How many times have you called a friend from the car to get directions to his home, but then couldn't tell him which direction you are going or what street you are on?

How do you get to Point B when Point A isn't even established? How are you going to get to financial abundance when you haven't decided what financial abundance means to you? Knowing where you stand financially and being honest with yourself is the first step. Then, you will have to be clear about what you want and expect to achieve. Finally, you need to know how you will get there.

Create a Vision

If you don't really know where you are going, it can be hard to move fast. Have you ever noticed how truly confident people walk quickly and forcefully toward their destination? People less sure of where they are headed will walk more hesitantly, stopping to look around for landmarks or meandering around without a sense of purpose.

We all have hopes and dreams, but for many of us, they are scattered. This leaves us fruitlessly working towards a bunch of ideas, but with no direct way of getting there. We exert energy and begin to feel as if our dreams are beyond our reach when the exact opposite is true.

Our dreams are achievable. Everything is possible when we develop a well-crafted plan. We should all craft a plan, map out their steps and directions and follow the course. We will work on developing the plan in depth over the course of the following chapters.

For now, give yourself free range to envision yourself wherever and however you would like to be. Put the book down for a moment and just daydream about the life you want to live or the money you would like to have.

Each individual's vision will be different. For some people, driving a sports car along the Pacific Coast Highway is the ultimate luxurious moment. For others, striding along a street in downtown Manhattan and heading to a steak dinner and a Broadway show is more important.

When you know your dream, keep it in mind as we work through this book.

When you are finished daydreaming, write down every detail of your vision. Be as creative as you can in describing your dream so that when you read it later you will be able to regain the same feeling you felt when you first had the dream. Visionaries like Jack Canfield often use this technique, calling it a dream board. With this activity, find pictures or create pictures of things that are part of your dream. By visualizing it, your chances of making it come true are better.

Start with Baby Steps

Now that you have your future visualized, you are ready to start moving toward your destination. If you don't know how to get there, you will fail. Some people can't "see the forest for the trees"; in other words, they focus on the details and not the overall picture. But other individuals have just the opposite personality: they can "see the forest but not the trees." When you daydream about the future, visualize a broad view of what your life will be like. But, in order to achieve your objectives, it's time to think on a smaller scale.

Think about other challenges you have set for yourself. Let's say you decided to train for a marathon, you didn't start on day one running twenty miles. Depending on your starting point, you may have run four or five miles the first day and then slowly and steadily increased your mileage until you reached your goal.

In order to succeed in anything you do, develop a plan, one based on the understanding that a series of small achievements are required before you can reach your most significant goal.

Financial abundance may not come to you on day one of your race, but it is achievable as long as you keep your list of positive affirmations near and maintain your focus on the future.

Conquer your Current Situation

The first baby step is to assess your current financial situation. We will focus on that topic in depth in later chapters. First understand that no matter what your current situation is or how long you think it will take to fix your financial missteps, you are ready to move toward your destination now. Don't wait until the timing is right, until you have found a better job or paid off your debts.

The time to start is now.

Spending time on your current situation may sound like something that will slow you down. It can make you feel as if your destination is out of reach. Learning how to cope with your current situation and facing the reality of your financial life are both part of the process which will move you closer to your destination. We won't be looking at the past. We will be looking at the future. But in order to do that, you must know where you stand today.

Do not allow yourself to put off making progress by offering excuses such as "I won't be able to do this" or "This will never happen to me." Many people want a better financial future, but they believe they are too deep in debt or too far behind others in terms of their income. In order to achieve great wealth you must believe in your own abilities. Take the struggle out of earning money and turn it into a challenge. Challenge yourself to reach the place you want to be financially.

There will be times when you are frustrated or feel as if everything is taking too long. You may feel it was foolish of you to believe you were capable of building prosperity for yourself and your family.

This path worked for me. I am delighted to show you how it will work for you.

The principles I have developed are not based on a whim or a dream.

This process works.

I know this because this is the process I used to rebuild my finances. It is the process I used to create a multi-million dollar business. I continue to use this process every day to sustain everything I have created.

There was a time when I was in an unhappy financial position. As I shared with you earlier, my life as an athlete ended abruptly when I was injured in a golf cart accident. While I was recovering in the hospital I was forced to face my dismal financial circumstances along with the challenge of physical therapy. I had to figure out a way to pull myself out of debt.

While I had been raised by a loving family and constantly encouraged by positive affirmations, my time in the hospital and in recovery were low points. I had doubts and fears about my financial future. Even though I had been raised to believe I could be anything I wanted and that I was destined for greatness, I had absolutely no idea how to get there. Doubts can flood in easily when you feel you are in a hopeless situation.

My family didn't let me stay for long in that place of doubt and fear. They talked sense into me and reminded me that everything is possible so I did not fall into a state of helplessness. I realized that if anything was going to change in my life, I was going to have to be the one to make the decisions. I knew that I would have to embrace the concept of change, learn to make wise decisions and implement those decisions in a way that would provide me with financial and emotional security. Little did I know that I was creating a process that would drastically change my life. Then it grew to change the lives of so many people.

I learned that I held the key to open any door I wanted.

The Outcome is Up to You

Now that you have listened to my story, it is time to start your own. You have decided to venture on a journey that will have a remarkable impact on your life. As you get started, keep in mind that you will need to rely on your belief in yourself and your efforts. While I will teach you in later chapters about how to build a support team, you must understand from the beginning the importance of maintaining your courage and your convictions. You can accomplish your dreams.

For inspiration, you may want to discuss your plans with close friends and family members. Choose a few people who you know want to see you succeed and share your strategy. Find the friends and family members who will be there to push you forward when you falter. Avoid spending time with people who are negative or are afraid you might fail. Even if their negativity is "well-meaning", you are looking to spend time with positive people right now.

Following your path to prosperity won't always be easy, but it won't always be hard, either. Use the resources around you for motivation, whether it comes from your group of friends or from the deep desire to pull yourself out from under the burden of debt. Whatever you need, use it to push yourself out of your situation and onto your destination.

Now that you have opened your mind to the possibility of an abundant future, we are ready to get started.

Remember, everything is possible.

PRINCIPLE ONE - MAKE WISE DECISIONS

Before we can move forward on any given day of our lives, we need to make dozens of decisions. Deciding what to have for breakfast may not have the major financial impact of deciding to buy a new car, yet each decision we make should be taken with care.

Generally, when we make a decision, we assume we are making a wise one. It is only later that we realize some of our choices have been mistakes, some choices were neutral, and other choices we have made turned out much better than expected. But just what is it that influences how we make choices? How can we shift the dynamic from a 50-50 chance at making a wise decision to making the right choice every time?

Each of the Prosperity Principles you learn in this book has value, but the first one is the most important: *Making Wise Decisions*. Without the underlying element of good judgment, the other Principles will be hard to follow.

To develop our decision-making skills, we begin by evaluating the decisions we have made in the past and determining how those decisions are impacting our life now. When we get lost, we ask for directions. In order to get to our destination, we must first figure out where we are. If you call a friend and ask for directions to their home, the first question they will ask is, "Where are you now?" You have to know exactly where you are before you get to where you are going!

You are going to begin a new phase in your life. This next phase is designed to build your personal prosperity. In order to do this right, we need to evaluate the decision-making style we use, especially when it comes to financial decisions. For some reason, many people never evaluate their decision making criteria. They just "make" a decision and go with it.

By evaluating the times we made good or prosperous decisions we can figure out how we did that. And then do it again. And again. And again. You will now be in a position to make consistently smart choices.

You may not like looking back at some of the choices you have made in the past that were painful, either in terms of your finances, or in your personal life. But this is one of the best places to review your decision making process. We often learn better from our failures than our successes. Reviewing choices we have made in the past that have hurt our finances or our personal lives can be painful, but by learning from our mistakes, we will avoid making bad decisions in the future.

Believe me I am speaking from experience. Even in my personal life, I caught myself making the same decisions over and over again. I dated a very prominent athlete for six years. We had many relationship woes. The typical issues, infidelity, respect, etc. However, when I was strong enough to get out of that relationship I found myself in several other dating scenarios with the exact same type of person.

Then my Mom read me a poem entitled "The Hole" by Portia Nelson. The first part of the poem speaks of me walking down a street with a deep hole that I fall into, leaving me lost and helpless. The next time, I walk down the same street, I pretend not to see the hole, and fall into it again, pretending that it couldn't be my fault. Yet again, I walk down the street, and this time, out of habit and through my own fault, I fall into the hole but am able to get out. The next time I walk down that street I avoid the hole. Finally, I learn to simply take a different street.

Making better decisions will change the path and direction of your future and eliminate the extreme negative effects of wrong thinking and wrong doing.

You will also begin to recognize patterns in your thinking and decision making processes. Your new goal is to approach your decision-making process with prosperity in mind. Not because something feels good. Not because your friend thinks it is a good idea. Not because you may have given someone your word some time back.

If your decision will not bring you closer to prosperity, it might not be the right decision. Every single decision we make, large or small, must be seen as a calculated move to get us closer to our goal: prosperity.

Emotional decisions about relationships with people can be messy and confusing because they may rely on a flawed understanding about the other person's motivations.

Financial decisions are usually more clear-cut (but not always).

For example, if you know that you need to invest a particular sum of money each month to reach your savings goal, it is usually obvious that an impulse buy of an expensive suit will undercut that goal. The wise decision in this case is to repress your emotional instinct and avoid unnecessary spending.

Intellectually, you know that investing $1000 will bring you more long-term rewards than purchasing a $1000 vacation. Emotionally, you still want it. This is the moment when a principled approach to decision-making should kick in and help you make a smart choice. Many people will give in to their impulse and buy that vacation, forgetting about their long-term vision. But if you are trained to make wise decisions and to recognize that EVERY decision can impact your ability to reach your goals, you are more likely to make the right choice.

Anyone who has worked with a personal trainer to reach their physical fitness goals knows that goals must be reached incrementally. On day one, you will start with day one exercises, and work yourself up to a fit and healthy lifestyle. You won't start with an advanced program that would only lead to failure. Reaching your fiscal fitness goals requires the same perseverance and incremental steps of a well-developed workout plan. As with any training, the process becomes easier over time. One wise decision (such as committing yourself to creating your own prosperity) will lead to another. By taking this one step at a time you are establishing a clear path to developing generational wealth for your family.

Review Your Decisions

We make dozens of decisions, hundreds...even thousands!

Some are minor decisions like, "What shoes do I wear today?" Or, "What should I eat for breakfast. These decisions may have an impact on your day. If you choose to wear high heels, but have an unexpectedly long day, your sore feet will complain about your decision. Or, if you chose to skip breakfast, but then found yourself missing lunch as well, you could be ravenous by dinnertime.

Bigger decisions, such as whether to invest in a particular opportunity or buy a particular home, will have a long-term impact. This type of decision far outreaches the effect felt whether you ate breakfast or wore high heels on any given day. If your investment goes bad, you could lose all your money or have it tied up in a venture that prevents you from investing in something more profitable. If you choose the wrong home you could be unhappy emotionally, physically, and financially. Those effects are far worse than a set of pinched toes or feeling hungry.

Not all outcomes of decision-making are negative. Plenty of them are positive. Your serendipitous choice of high heels could have worked out for the best if it turned out you had a last-minute invitation to cocktail party after work. Your investment could turn out to double or triple your money. Perhaps skipping breakfast left you plenty hungry for a power luncheon you might otherwise have begged off where you met a new client who could bring very desirable business your way.

The point of training yourself to make wise decisions is to increase the likelihood that your choices will have positive outcomes and decrease the chances of negative consequences. Some decisions are pure chance. The idea behind evaluating decisions is to minimize chance or risk from your decision-making process.

Where Are You Today?

Wherever you are in your life right now is based on the impact of every decision you have ever made.

- Did you choose to go to college?
- What career path did you choose?
- Where do you live?
- Did you get married?
- Did you choose to start a family?
- At what age did you do all these things?
- Have you saved money?
- Have you invested money?

All these choices impact where you are now.

Financial decisions, in particular, will impact your ability to move toward your goal of prosperity. While the focus of this book is toward prosperity, you can use the same principles to make all kinds of decisions in your life.

Look at where you are now. You haven't always made the best decisions, have you? That's normal. We all do that, making some good decisions and some poor decisions. I haven't always made the best decisions. I had to train myself to make consistently better, more prosperous decisions, and learn from the past mistakes.

And this is something we can all do.

Now turn to the exercise section at the back of this book. (Exercise 1) The exercise will help you evaluate your decisions, look at some of the bad decisions you have made in the past and think of some better choices that might have had different outcomes.

There may be nothing you can do about lost money from a bad investment. But, by evaluating where your decision-making criteria went wrong, you will be in a better position to visualize the possibility of future, successful investments. Don't focus on the bad outcomes of some of your earlier decisions. Focus on how you made the decision, and make a conscious decision to change that. Stay positive about your potential and know that you are going to make great decisions moving forward!

What would your life look like once you consistently make wise decisions? Wouldn't the quality of your life improve?

This is the best news you've heard all day: Decision-making is a skill that can be learned and enhanced.

Yes! You can train your mind just as you train your body. Just as you go to the gym and do all your exercises the right way to develop and tone your muscles, you can practice the right way to make your decisions. By repeating these steps over and over when you make future decisions, your life will turn prosperous.

One of the best ways you can positively change your decision-making habits is to not make a bad decision.

Easier said than done, right?

Wrong!

When you find yourself making a decision similar to one you have made before, stop and think.

- What happened the last time?
- Did you take everything into consideration?
- Were you satisfied with the outcome of your previous decision?
- If you weren't satisfied with the outcome, why would you do it again?

Repeating our mistakes means we haven't evaluated them properly. We're reacting to a situation, not acting with careful consideration. Repeating our mistakes over and over hoping for a different outcome meets the definition of insanity.

Making wise decisions can be challenging, especially when that decision involves money. Sometimes we want to take the easy way out, even when it may not be the best choice. Many times, the instant gratification we get from an impulse purchase or a snap decision will result in long-term regret. Just ask those around you who are drowning in credit card debt.

Training your mind to see beyond the moment and into the future can exponentially improve your quality of life in the years to come.

The "basic training" aspect of wise decision–making relies on learning from our past mistakes. When we choose to do things differently than we have in the past, we are on the road to making wiser decisions.

What do you feel when you think about starting your own business? Many people feel fear. We will discuss the role fear plays in decision-making soon, but for now just remember that we should never make a decision when we are feeling fear.

What do you feel about investing? You might just feel more comfortable in the beginning by putting your credit cards away and not shopping.

Changing your decision-making patterns to achieve better results is what wise decision-making is all about. Using your past habits as an example of what **NOT** to do will help you move forward and make wiser decisions.

Wisdom is applied knowledge.

Using careful judgment for new decisions along with experiences from your past can increase your chances of making the right decision. Now that we know we have to make good quality, educated decisions let's talk about the types of decisions we may face.

Learning to Make Decisions

Just as we learn anything, we can learn to make better decisions or choices in our life. Here is the Eight-Step Decision-Making Process that I use every day. It took me years to develop this. Hopefully it will save you years of time and a great deal of money. I have broken the eight steps into two parts. Part I deals with understanding the decision you are about to make. Part II deals with actually making the decision.

Part I: UNDERSTANDING THE DECISION
Step One: What Type of Decision is it?

While the wise decision-making process applies to any and every decision, we should take a minute to point out that there are generally three types of decisions.

The Yes/No Decision. A Yes/No decision sounds very simple, doesn't it? The answer is either yes or no. Don't let the simplicity of this question fool you. Answering the question, "Should I invest in this opportunity?" should be thoughtfully considered.

The Options Decision. These questions have a variety of answers and naturally lend themselves to careful consideration. "Which investment should I choose? How much should I invest in any one type of project? Should I take my friend's advice and invest along with them?"

The "Only If" Decision. This decision depends on particular circumstances, such as "I will only invest in that particular venture only if I can make a twenty percent return." This type of decision requires significant research first, and then depends on your judgment.

While each of these decisions is a different type of decision, the approach to take with each of them is similar.

Every choice you make should be based on your goals.

Step Two: The Four Ways Decisions Are Made

One way to improve your decision-making ability is to track the way you have made decisions in the past. Do you tend to operate on intuition? Or do you follow a leader or a mentor and make your decisions based on that person's past decisions or what you perceive would be their choices now?

A common practice for most people is to make a decision based on **feelings;** that old "gut feeling" or using your "intuition." Without gathering any information that can provide ballast for a sound choice, we listen to our hearts and not our heads. When we use intuition in making our decisions we are throwing your chances to the wind and choosing to let go of our control over the outcome. Everyone opts to "go with their gut" at one time or another. I've even used this method in the past. I just would never recommend this as a viable decision-making option because the potential consequences are too volatile. Frankly, I consider this a lazy way of making a decision since no effort is exerted.

The second decision-making process is to follow **patterns.** Individuals often make a decision in the same way they always have. Either they are following the decision-making methods taught by their parents or their mentors or they are simply following their own habits (many of these habits are bad habits). If we never try to change the way you make choices, we will simply keep going in a circle and never break free.

The third way many people make choices is to **follow** the actions or advice of a friend. "My friend did it this way, so I will too." Your teammate opted to invest in a local ice cream shop, so you put your money in it, too. You did not research or investigate if this choice was a good one for you, but it worked for them so it should work for you, too. This is a pretty lazy way of making decisions.

The fourth way to make a decision uses the **logical method**. When you use logic to make choices, you weigh your options, view the pros and cons and make sure you get your desired result. The logical method is an educated approach that allows us the greatest possibility of achieving the outcome we desire.

Using logic is the way you should train your mind to make *all* decisions.

Wise decision-making relies on you making good judgments.

When you find yourself having to make a decision, and you feel rushed, or aren't sure why you're making the decision…STOP! Think about it first.

What kind of decision are you making?
- Yes/No
- An option
- Only If

Next, ask yourself how you usually make decisions.
- Feelings
- Patterns
- Follow the leader
- Using logic

We already know that we have to use logic to make our choice. So analyze the situation. Evaluate the pros and cons. What is the anticipated outcome of each of your choices?

Now, make a decision based on the outcome that brings you closer to your long-term goals. This slow and thoughtful approach will prevent making bad decisions.

Every decision should be based on two main elements:
1. Keeping your long-term plan in mind.

2. Seeking out as much information as you can to make your choice based on facts rather than emotion.

Step Three: Why Am I Making This Decision?

Keeping the end result in mind is key to your success. When you make choices, this helps to keep the picture clear in your mind. Positive affirmations and visualizations work well to develop a big picture outlook on decision-making.

Emotional Unattachment

Did you know we usually make wiser and better decisions for others than we do for ourselves? We certainly do. And it is because we are *emotionally unattached* to the outcome of our decision.

The next time you face a decision, detach your emotions. If necessary, pretend you are making this decision for someone else who won't take any excuses if the result is bad.

Details are the Key

Now it is time to develop a more detailed blueprint of the decision you need to make. In order to make a wise decision, start by being honest with yourself and developing a plan.

Slow down.

While your excitement at the idea of building prosperity is an important element in moving forward, you also must train your mind to take the time to think through every decision carefully.

In real estate, this process is known as **due diligence**. Step back and review everything surrounding the decision you are about to make. Some questions to ask yourself as you embark on a new decision include:

- How would I advise someone else about this decision?
- What would my advice be?
- Can I make a decision to follow my own advice?
- Can I sell this decision to someone else?

"The devil is in the details."

This old saying means that small things in our plans that are overlooked may cause serious problems later. Each decision you make can have immediate effects. It will likely have long-term effects as well. What might seem like a small decision could have huge ramifications!

Let's say you choose to buy that $1000 vacation I mentioned earlier, you will have the instant impact of enjoying a good time. You will also notice an immediate drop in your bank account balance. If you have chosen to charge the purchase on your credit card, you will see that balance and the resulting increase in your minimum payment.

Both of these are clues you use in future choices. The outcome of your decision, good or bad, affects you now and in the future. The long-term impact won't be felt as quickly or as easily, yet that is the outcome that could have the biggest effect on your life.

If, instead of spending $1000 on a vacation, you put that money in a savings account or a money market account, you would be earning interest that would increase the value of the money over time. For example, that $1000 would become $1340 if you invested it in an account earning 6% for five years. Matching the $1000 with additional funds to make a down payment on a home or to make another investment could bring far larger rewards than the pleasure afforded by a vacation.

Giving in to the temptation of the vacation could result in a setback to achieving your financial goals. Short-term, you will have spent money to satisfy an emotional need. Long-term, you will have postponed your commitment to your goal of prosperity.

Splurging for a vacation requires less detailed decision-making than a major investment such as purchasing a house. One of my clients initially thought he needed to decide whether he should buy an older, fixer-upper single family home or a new townhouse.

I suggested he step back to evaluate the broader implications of his decisions.

He realized there were many decisions to be made before he was ready to choose which house to purchase.

- First, he needed to evaluate whether it made more sense for him to buy a home or to rent one.
- He needed to think about his intentions for the future, and more importantly, the market conditions of that particular city.
  - Was he going to want to live in that city for years to come?

- Was this going to be an easy home to sell or rent if he wanted to leave?
- Is the city growing and was this a good time in the Real Estate market to purchase?
- Will this home appreciate or at lease hold its value?
- Then personally, was there job stability and will this home sustain a growing family?

Bottom line...Does this purchase really make sense?

Once my client had decided that purchasing a home was the right move for him now, he could now focus his attention on *which* home to buy.

As you can see, details were at the crux of the choice. Here were other questions he asked himself once he realized that this decision was anything but simple:

- Was it financially wise to own a fixer upper?
- Which home would cost him more money in the long run?
- Will the difference in the price between the older home and the more expensive newer home still be significant once the cost of fixing the older home is included?
- Which home will create more of an asset?

Every wise decision requires answers to questions and more questions before we can reach the best conclusion.

Research

Every wise decision is based on facts.

While you will use your judgment to evaluate those facts, first comes a bit of research. This research will help you estimate every possible outcome to each decision.

In the example of the home purchase, a good and honest question-and-answer session with yourself is a GREAT place to start. Questions will arise that need to be researched to obtain correct answers.

Start by making a list of the information you need and questions to be answered before you can make an informed decision.

WRITE THEM DOWN!!!

We would like to believe that we will remember everything, but we don't. Keep a written record. I've often thought of a really great question, but if I didn't write it down, it was lost.

What information is important? What do you need to know to make a good and successful decision?

Research.

Fact find.

Do your *due diligence.*

When deciding whether you are ready to buy your first home or not, arm yourself with a lot of information. Use the following four steps to gather that information:

Step 1: Start with your personal finances:

- Gather all your financial paperwork and review it to get an accurate picture of how much cash you have for a down payment and how much you can comfortably afford to spend on your monthly housing payments.
- Evaluate your monthly budget to see if there are places you can spend less money so that you can save more.
- Request your free annual credit report and study it so you can correct any errors or find a way to improve your credit score.

In the back of this book you will see an example of a detailed balance sheet. (Exercise 2) **USE IT!** Make copies and do this once a year. This will show you **EXACTLY** where you are financially and you will be able to track your progress.

Remember, knowing where you are is the first step in getting to where you want to be.

Step 2: Meet With a Mortgage Lender:
- After you have researched your own finances meet with a lender who can talk with you about qualifying for a mortgage. There are many good lenders and many bad ones so get a few recommendations and before anyone starts pulling your credit give them ALL of the facts you already have, including your credit score.
- Ask for rates and pricing and compare your lenders. There is nothing wrong with letting them fight over your business. Make them give you a deal!

Step 3: Work with a Knowledgeable Real Estate Agent:

- Working with a knowledgeable local Real Estate agent can educate you about what types of homes are available in your price range.
- Choose your Real Estate agent wisely. All Real Estate agents are not created equal. Just because your sister's husband's sister's best friend is a Real Estate agent does not make them the best or most knowledgeable choice for you. Not all agents do all types of real estate. As a matter of fact **no** agent does **everything**. There are seller's agents, and buyer's agents, and agents that strictly work with real estate investments.
- Remember, they are making money so don't let them just tell you what you want to hear. Make them prove it. Interview them and make an educated decision on your needs as to who the best agent for you may be.

Step 4: Do Your Due Diligence:

- Internal research needs to be done, during which you will need to carefully think about your future plans including your job, potential changes in your family size and your commitment to staying in one location for years to come. This substantive research is a necessary step before you can even begin to make a decision on buying a home.
- Once your research has been completed, you will need to determine the outcome that will make you happy and put you on the path towards success. What do you hope to accomplish with this decision? What does the decision look like in the end? Be clear about your desired end result. Be careful to consider every possible outcome of your decision.

- Make sure the choice you are making eliminates any issues that may arise.
- Work backwards from your goal before you make a final decision to make sure you are not missing any potential alternative choices or outcomes.
- Look into alternatives. The more alternatives you have, the easier it will be to see the many directions your decisions could take. Look at your decision from every angle. Ask yourself, "What will happen if I decide this way? How will the outcomes differ if I chose to do one thing rather than another?" Ask as many questions as you can about each decision. You can even ask others what they would do in order to get different views on the decision. But be careful. Wise decisions should always be made by you in light of your research and judgment, not someone else.

Risk

After you have analyzed the decision, go back one more time to review your options.

This time, *focus on risk.*

Think about every possible risk associated with the decision you are about to make. An organized decision-maker will pull out pen and paper and write down all the pros and cons of each option. Look at the list very carefully.

- Do the cons outweigh the pros?
- Are the pros more important to you?
- Assess your risk accordingly.
- Evaluate the consequences of failure.
- Will failure be life changing?

- Will success be life changing?

Establishing a Powerful Mind: Assumptions, Opinions, and Stress

Making wise decisions naturally requires time and careful thought. Paying attention to our thoughts and how we let them affect our decisions can make or break our decisions.

Our minds control what we do.

But, we can train our minds to focus on positive thinking.

Remember the positive affirmations you developed in the introduction to this book? Pull out that list again, (it should be copied into the back of this book.)

These positive affirmations are designed to diminish your negative thoughts about money.

But positive thinking doesn't have to focus solely on money. Do the same thing with negative views you have about anything and turn them into positives.

For example, I could have chosen to let life defeat me when I had my golf cart accident. I was in the hospital for six months and rehab and physical therapy for another six months. I could have said, "Well… those were just the cards I was dealt." However, when the doctor told me there was a possibility of losing my foot and never running again, I chose to believe otherwise. Lying in that hospital bed, I resolved to not only walk out of that hospital with my foot, I would run again.

Today, I run all three of my dogs on a daily basis and you would never even know I was in an accident.

Whenever you find yourself thinking negatively about a decision, stop. Put that decision aside until you are in a better frame of mind. Decisions should be made only when you are ready to focus on outcomes rather than emotions. Making a decision when you're feeling emotional or particularly negative wastes all the energy you put into your research.

One way to establish your mindset is to be constantly vigilant and observant of your thoughts. Always consider which thoughts you are letting into your mind, especially when you are making a decision, then be extremely careful of the words you allow to come out of your mouth. What you say is what you believe in your heart and it will come to pass. From the heart our mouths speak. Our tongues are like ships rudders. The smallest part of the ship steers its direction and destiny. Life and death are truly in the power of the tongue.

There may be times when you find yourself making a decision based on long-held **assumptions** instead of your research. It is natural to think these assumptions are correct just because you have thought that way for such a long time. If you haven't done any research on a topic, be sure you stop assuming you know something about it.

For example, perhaps you have heard that real estate investors are making piles of money. You've have one more lousy day at your crappy job. Rather than researching and making an educated decision to get into real estate investing, you quit your job and go and buy a fixer-upper to flip. If you haven't done your due diligence and understand what it takes to be a successful real estate investor, you're doomed to failure.

You made a decision based on an assumption…not on fact.

Sure, some people can get lucky, but most of the time a decision based on assumption rather than fact is not the way to ensure future success.

When you find yourself basing your decision on an assumption, *STOP!*

Go back to your research and do your due diligence. The assumption isn't necessarily false, but make sure you take the time to determine the facts. If your assumption is correct, you can move forward. If it is wrong, then throw out that assumption and use other facts to make your decision.

Assumptions have an equally nefarious companion…*opinions. Everyone* has *opinions.* Sometimes our opinions get in the way of making a wise decision, but other times they support a good decision.

Where did your opinion come from? They could be based on your values, in which case you should listen. If the opinion is based on hearsay or other the opinions of other people, you may need to step back and make sure you are thinking objectively.

Stress is one more factor that keeps many people from making a wise decision. Stress negatively impacts our ability to think, interferes with our concentration and hinders us from recognizing pertinent facts and from seeing all our options.

If you find yourself making a decision during a stressful situation, take the time out to sleep on it. If you don't have time for a full night's sleep before you must make a choice, at least take a moment or a breather to step away from the stress. Take a walk around the block or even around the office to give yourself time to think.

Wise decisions take time.

If your mind is affected by stress, negative thoughts or assumptions without a basis in fact, take a moment to remind yourself that these are bad habits that should be broken.

Focus on the positive methods you have learned and then confirm that your decision is a wise one.

Know Yourself and Your Goals

Goals are the key to success.

It has been proven that people who write down their goals have a far greater success rate than those who just keep their goals in their mind.

In order to achieve everything you desire, ***write down your goals!*** Then figure out how to make that goal a reality. What steps will you take? What actions? What obstacles must you overcome? This is how to make a dream a reality.

Goals →→Decisions→→ Thoughts→→ Action

An exercise that will help you organize your goals can be found in the Exercises chapter at the back of this book. (Exercise3)

After you have outlined your goals, develop a detailed blueprint of the decisions you must now make. This is your road map, your daily guide for what you are doing and how you will get there. All of your choices should line up with your goals.

Don't skip the important step of writing down your goals. Look at your goals every day in order to remind yourself of your objectives.

A wise decision will not be the same decision for every individual. Just as each person has different goals, each decision will be a reflection of the person making the choice. Before you can make a wise decision, know who you are, what is important to you and what you want in the short-term and the long-term.

Many decisions fall through or don't produce the expected outcome because the person making the decision is not certain of what he really wants. Be the guide to your own destination.

Remember when we talked about asking for directions earlier in this chapter? When your friend asks "where are you now?" you need that information at your fingertips. Each of us must be clear on exactly where we are and what our end destination is before we can establish a clear route to where we are going. When you write down your affirmations, your vision for your future and your specific goals, you are planning your route just as you would plan a road trip with your friends.

No matter what your goals are, have a clear vision of the outcome and the steps to take to get from Point A to Point B.

For instance, some people think joining a gym to get in shape is a wise decision, a good way to spend money. A gym membership can be valuable, but only for people who have a well-established plan. If you join a gym to just "get in shape", how will you know when you have reached your objective? Setting specific a goal, such as lowering your cholesterol by fifty points or losing twenty pounds or gaining the stamina to play a full set of tennis with your teenage son, means you will know when you have achieved your objective. You will also need to know where you are now – your cholesterol, your weight or how long you can stay on the tennis court without collapsing.

The concept here is simple: know what you want, know where you are, and then take the necessary steps and make the wise decisions to reach your goal.

It's up to you.

You are the one who can choose to go wherever you want to go. Everything is possible. However, if your destination or the outcome you are looking for is constantly shifting, you may find that your decisions will not produce your desired goals.

Clarity

Success requires clarity.

You have to be clear about where you are and where you are going. This will help you make a strong decision, and make it easier for you to put trust in your decision. One way to develop clarity is to put not only your goals but also your values in writing.

When you see a list of what matters most to you in life you will be able to keep long-term goals in perspective.

Values

Your values are what make you "tick."

They are why you do the things you do and they explain the decisions you make.

Because of this, part of the decision making process has to do with values. Knowing your values helps you gain clarity and focus, but ultimately you must use that newfound clarity to make consistent decisions and take committed action.

The whole point of discovering your values is to improve the results you get in those areas that are most important to you. Values establish how you spend your time, your money, and your energy.

In the Exercises section at the back of the book is a simple exercise that can help you clearly establish your values and your priorities (Exercise 4). When you have completed that exercise you will probably find that you wrote your goals to reflect your values.

It took me two hours to do this exercise and rationalize why I was making certain choices. You may be shocked at what you come up with.

I was.

From the start I would have said my number one value was spirituality. No one could have made me think differently. When I did the exercise, my number one value was loyalty. My rationalization was that if you are not loyal to your belief system and those around you, you will not be loyal to your spirituality. My top six values really represented who I was, and the order I put them in made sense in my mind. In my thought process every other value on the list fit somewhere in the top six I had chosen. Do yours and hold on to them. Think about your values the next time you find yourself making a decision.

Now look at your goals and your values side by side. (Exercise 5)

Do they line up?

If not, rearrange your goals and put them in order starting with what is most important to your values and to you. This will help establish who you truly are and will help guide you in every decision you make.

You will find clarity once you recognize what is truly significant in your life.

You may not have been aware of this until now, but your values should influence every decision you make. The main benefit of knowing your values is that you will gain tremendous clarity and focus. Ultimately, you will use that newfound clarity to make consistent decisions and take committed action.

The whole point of discovering your values is to improve the results you get in those areas that are truly most important to you. Values are priorities that tell you how to spend your time, your money, and your energy. Think about your values as you make decisions. Your list of values should visually demonstrate to you what holds precedence in your life. Anything that has significance in your life should be consistent with your values and should be part of the choices that you made when creating your list. If family comes first for you, then tailor your objectives to meet the needs of your family.

Once you have your values in writing it will be easier to match your decisions to meet your objectives and keep them in line with your values. Making wise decisions will be easier when you understand the underlying values and motivations that are driving you to your destination.

Step Four: Is Something Worrying Me About This Decision?

Why Am I Worried or Afraid?

Never make a decision in fear.

Fear will always cause you to make the wrong choices. People who fear failure often choose not to do anything to move their lives forward.

But, not doing anything is a decision in itself!

Some people fear success as much as they fear failure because they cannot imagine how they will handle success. Making a decision based on your fear of failure or your fear of success could result in an irrational decision.

Sometimes people are so afraid to find out what the outcome will be of their decision that they make themselves sick or are unable to sleep. As soon as you find yourself becoming emotionally and perhaps physically scared about your options, you will lose your ability to think clearly.

If you usually make decisions based on your gut instinct or by following your old patterns, using the wise decision-making process may be disconcerting or even frightening. Plenty of people go through life by making as few decisions as possible, allowing others to make their choices for them or just coasting along until, by default, an option is chosen. Making the choice to use the wise decision-making process is an important step to take and a wise decision in itself.

Opting to make careful, educated judgments comes naturally to some people, but for others, this new approach can create uncertainty. The more personal a decision is, the harder it may be to remain objective. This is particularly true of decisions that could result in instant happiness but perhaps long-term regret.

There are ways to overcome the inclination to revert to your old ways by opting for an instinctive decision.

Recognize fear. Ask yourself what you are afraid of and research what will help you make an educated, wise decision.

Recognize that you are facing a challenge to your old habits. Sometimes all it takes to change your mindset is to give yourself a pat on the back for making an effort to improve your habits.

Be Honest

Be honest with yourself.

Acknowledge your discomfort with the decision you are about to make. Recognize the fear you feel, and then ask yourself, "What is it that is worrying me? Am I afraid of the outcome? Am I afraid of trying something new? Am I uncomfortable with making this type of decision?

Write down your feelings. Once you get your concerns on paper, you can more easily understand exactly what is keeping you from making the best decision.

Expect a Challenge

When we talk about the process of making wise decisions, we may believe that we can always expect a positive outcome. This would be impossible, given the reality of life. So be prepared for the unexpected. In the time period between the moment you make a decision and the realization of the result of that decision, it is natural to worry. Just recognize that there will always be bumps in the road and that every bump can mean another opportunity.

Turning the negative into a positive is part of the process.

By now you know my story. I turned getting run over by a golf cart and almost losing my foot into a time to redirect my life, study real estate, and learn all I could while I was hospitalized and bed-ridden.

Challenges give you the opportunity to develop stories of triumph.

I tell my TEAM, the problem solvers will always rise to the top. Most people dwell on the problem. Not you, not anymore. Listen to the challenge or problem and respond with a wise, educated solution.

Become your own problem-solver.

Stay Positive

Remember my opening words to this book?

"Everything is possible."

If you begin to doubt yourself and your decisions, go back and review the positive affirmations you wrote in the back of this book, your vision for the future, your list of goals and your notes on which decisions from your past could have been better. Each of these tools will help you move past fear, push worry aside and stay focused on your plans.

Don't allow your fears and worries to be a roadblock to your success. Push past the challenge of negative feelings and reinvigorate your positive outlook. Use your apprehension to become stronger in the face of adversity. Overcoming obstacles should be an opportunity for growth.

Stay Focused

Keep your commitment to success.

The easy path would be to give in to your feelings, to become distracted by "what if" questions and to lose sight of your goals.

Clearly state to yourself, either verbally or in writing, what may be bothering you once you have made a decision. Address the problem directly and recognize the futility of time spent worrying and rethinking a choice to which you are committed.

If you stay strong and keep your intentions in front of you, then fear cannot stop you.

Try this trick used by dieters and by home-based salespeople: put a photo on your refrigerator that represents your goal. Visualizing your goal (a house, a car or maybe even a full bank account) daily will remind you why you embarked on this new decision-making process.

Ignore Negativity

Any time you try something new, you may find that your friends and family or colleagues are not as supportive as you would like them to be.

When you have made an effort to make a wise decision and used the decision making process you must rely on your own judgment and ignore any negativity that surrounds you. Some readers may be lucky enough or have chosen friends so well that they are embraced by a strong support system of people who will provide only positive feedback for their wise decisions.

For many people, though, beginning a new phase of decision-making will require an inner strength because they are surrounded by people who try to talk them out of their ideas, decisions, or plans. Most of the time, these negative people have a misplaced sense of protection. "I don't want to see you lose your hard-earned money on investing in real estate." Most of the time, negative people have a lot of opinions about things that they are not experts. (And you remember what I said about opinions, don't you?)

Remain true to your vision and your decisions and disregard any negative messages or expectations around you. Recognize the value in the decisions you make as they lead you toward your goals. Realize that by taking steps to ensure that you don't repeat past mistakes you are getting closer to your dreams.

Negative feelings may arise within your own mind as well as from other people, particularly when you are inexperienced at making wise decisions. Confidence comes with time, practice, and with the knowledge that you have made a choice based on information and judgment. As you continue to make wise decisions, your confidence will grow and good decision making becomes easy and habitual.

Step Five: Ask the Four Questions:

Now that you have learned how to make a wise decision, it is time to start making some decisions that will lead you closer to your goal. Begin by being aware of the everyday decisions you make and thinking about how they will affect you long-term.

Ask yourself the following four simple questions every time you make even the smallest choice:

1. Will this purchase or decision help me get to my destination?
2. Have I given this decision enough thought?
3. Have I done my research on every option of my decision?
4. Does it line up with my goals and values?

If you answer "no" to any of the questions above, then you should say "no" to your decision. Start by using these four simple questions with easy decisions such as buying a latte, shopping for shoes, or even picking up a few groceries. Look at this as a challenge. Take a note card and write these four questions on it and use them until this becomes habitual.

The process of asking these four questions *every time* you make a decision will make you more conscious of your decision-making habits. It will train your mind to think more about every decision rather than allowing emotion to rule your choices.

A great example of asking these questions is a trip to the grocery store where shoppers are notorious for making impulse buys. This is especially true if they shop when they are hungry or neglect to make a list. Next time you are in the supermarket, use the four-question process to decide whether you should purchase each item in your cart. Then, focus hard on price comparisons. Make sure you are comparing prices per ounce and not being taken in by bargains on items you won't use.

You are likely to find your typical grocery bill cut in half!

Once you have conquered being more aware of decision-making, you will naturally begin applying the process to every choice you make.

Wise Decision-Making Outline

We've gone over the eight steps to making a wise decision in great detail. Here is the same material in outline form. Copy this outline and keep it with you. This will help you to memorize the material and remember how to make a wise decision every time.

Part I: UNDERSTANDING THE DECISION
Step One: What Type of Decision is it?
1. Yes/no Decision
2. Options Decision
3. Only If Decision

Step Two: The Ways Decisions Are Made
1. Intuition (No)
2. Pattern (No)
3. Follow (No)
4. Logical (Yes)

Step Three: Why Am I Making This Decision?
Details are the Key
Research
Risk

Establishing a Powerful Mind: Assumptions, Opinions, and Stress
Know Yourself and Your Goals
Clarity
Values

Step Four: Is Something Worrying Me About This Decision?
Why Am I Worried or Afraid?
Be Honest
Expect a Challenge
Stay Positive
Stay Focused

Step Five: Ask the four questions
1. Will this purchase or decision help me get to my destination?
2. Have I given this decision enough thought?
3. Have I done my research on every option of my decision?
4. Does it line up with my goals and values?

Part II: MAKING THE DECISION
Step Six: Research the Facts
Establish your Goals
Establish your Values
Set Your Criteria
Develop Alternatives
Assess the Risk

Step Seven: Be Clear About What to Decide

Step Eight: Know What Kind Of Result You Want
(Exercise 6:)

There will be times when it is impossible to gather everything you want to know.

Do NOT let this paralyze you! Instead, make a decision based on the information you *are* able to collect. Research as much as you can until it is time to make a decision. As time permits, continue to think about the decision at hand. List as many options as you can, making each option as precise as possible. The more options you have available, the easier it will be to make a wise decision.

Dedicate yourself to making the decision and then do it.

If your decision doesn't bring you the outcome you planned, adjust your choice until it does. There are times when good decisions may end up having bad outcomes.

I have always lived by the adage:

Make a decision.
If you don't like it, make a *new* one.

You are in control. When you see that a decision isn't going as planned, reevaluate, adapt, and then move on.

When you are in the reevaluation process, go back to your written notes and see what has changed or what outcomes were unexpected. Write down the issues you are wrestling with to gain clarity. An important element of wise decision-making is to leave behind the bad habit of negative thinking and move forward into a world of positive actions and abundance.

Decision-making impacts every single part of our lives, which is why correctly implementing a process to make smart choices is both important and difficult. You have already learned a lot by reading this chapter.

Now it is time to put the process into practice.

The more opportunities you have to apply these decision-making tools, the more quickly you will grow from novice to expert decision-maker. Practice makes perfect.

No matter how much confidence you may have in your ability to make strong choices, you should still take the decision-making process step by step. Make sure you remember to collect facts before you make a choice.

You may be tempted to consult people you might consider to be experts regarding the decision you are making. Be sure to dissect the reason for someone's opinion. It could be that their situation is different from yours or the outcome they are looking for is not what you want. Seek the advice of experts but always compare their approach to yours. At the end of the day, every decision is up to you.

You know your needs better than anyone.

You understand your abilities better than anyone.

You have a specific goal in mind.

Stress and Decision-Making

Make sure you realize the negative impact stress can have on your decision-making. When you are overwhelmed by emotion or even just overtired you won't be at your peak for decision-making. Wait until your stress and emotion are under control before moving forward.

Of course, time is often a factor in decision-making. The timing of a decision may not always be in your control, and this can be stressful. If you can choose a timeframe before making a decision, make sure you allow yourself the time to complete the entire process. But, it will be a very rare occasion when you will be able to take all the time required to be as detailed as you want when making a decision. Try to control your timing as much as possible and allow yourself the freedom of time when you can. Don't be held hostage by it.

Commit Yourself

Follow through. Make it a habit to stand by each decision and see it through until you have reached the outcome you want. Training your mind to make a decision is valuable; but the follow through on every decision is what will bring you prosperity.

Now that you understand how to make wise decisions, the time has come to commit yourself to each and every decision you make. My mother always told me to make a decision, evaluate the outcome, and COMMIT. Remember my Little League experience? I'd made a decision, and my mother forced me to commit. I didn't exactly evaluate the outcome that time, but the next time you can be sure I did!

If you make a wrong decision, then learn from it and make a better one next time. Don't be afraid to make a decision and stick with it. But if you realize that you have made a mistake, your next step is to follow the wise decision-making process and correct it.

Your confidence will soar as you make better and better decisions based on the tools you have been given. Now it is time to re-commit yourself to your goals.

PRINCIPLE TWO – LEAD YOUR WEALTH

Now that you have learned to make wise decisions and are putting your newfound knowledge into practice, it is time to focus on using your decision-making ability to achieve your financial goals. In order to do that we must conquer fear, create a financial plan, and begin to implement that plan.

Develop some skills so that you can properly control your finances. While you must control your own finances, you will likely require a team unless you are a financial advisor and/or a real estate investment expert already. In order to properly hire these experts for your team I will teach you how to find the right experts, how to figure out if they are the right advisor for you. Finally, when you have identified the right advisor(s) for your team, we'll talk about how to move forward with your team in place.

This chapter is *not* meant to be skimmed. Far too many people have allowed their financial advisor to advise them right into the poor house. Doing your homework here at the beginning of your Prosperity Journey means you will know where your money is and what it is doing for you. This chapter will help to identify the best advisors for this important journey, but you are the one in control.

This may be the beginning of your financial education. Do NOT cede this important task to someone else.

Controlling Your Finances Requires a Team Effort

Control Your Own Finances

We need discipline in order to make wise decisions. We need discipline to control our time. And, we need discipline to control our emotions. Without discipline, the chances of achieving any goal are slim.

You want to build financial security for yourself and your family. This requires that you discipline your time, your emotions, and your finances.

As we begin to build wealth, we must educate ourselves about the process. Then we develop a team of support professionals to guide us. The key word here is "support". No matter how much or how little experience you have with investing and making financial decisions, you must be the person to know where your money is at all times and to make the final decision on everything.

Never turn your finances over to someone else to manage.

Even if you are a beginning investor in real estate or stocks, only you can be the leader of your own destiny.

Having total control over your finances doesn't mean that you have to do everything yourself. It does mean that you must always stay completely involved with every financial decision rather than trusting someone else to make decisions for you.

You must lead your own wealth.

While it is still essential to have the guidance of experts, you don't give over complete control over your finances and decisions that need to be made. There are plenty of examples in recent years of celebrities, who have sometimes made millions only to find themselves penniless and owing hundreds of thousands of dollars to the IRS or to creditors because they made terrible financial choices and allowed someone else total control over their money. These celebrities are no different from ordinary individuals who choose to allow others to make their decisions for them, it's just that when a celebrity falls from grace and into financial ruin, everyone hears about it.

I am a firm believer in financial advisors. But you must be in control of your advisor rather than allowing your advisor to be in control of you. Let your advisor suggest, let him sell you on why that stock or investment or property purchase is wise. Research it. Ask other financially educated people for their opinion. Find out what the benefit or gain is for you if you make the investment and what the gain will be for your financial advisor. Is the investment transparent? Can you see all aspects of the deal? Where is everyone expecting to make their money?

All the knowledge that you have acquired about making wise decisions can help you make the right choices when it comes to your finances. Remember one of the most important steps of making wise decisions: do your due diligence.

You don't have to go to graduate school and get a degree in investment banking. It simply means that you must ask questions of the experts you trust until you understand the suggestions they are making.

Building Your Team

While you ought to be in control of your money, no one expects you to be a genius. This is where your new decision-making skills come into play. You must use them to find trustworthy and skilled people who can help you to build your wealth.

Many consumers opt to work with a financial advisor or a financial consultant, but not everyone needs to begin with a financial advisor. A financial advisor is an important component to building your wealth, but the most important component is YOU!

The key to leading your wealth is to be aware of where your money is invested and how it is performing. The more knowledge you gain, the better your trust will be in yourself and the better your relationship will be with your financial advisor.

As you learn more about investing in the stock market, bonds, and real estate, you will be able to recommend certain ventures to your financial advisors and get their advice on it rather than expecting them to know the best recommendation for you. When you feel in control of your money you can make confident decisions about your future.

There are no self-made millionaires.

Yes, I actually said that.

Regardless of what people do or how they have made money, every wise and successful business person has a TEAM. You are now in charge of putting together your team. You want to surround yourself with people who are essential to your success. You can have a great idea but without backend support you will never succeed.

As your money grows, you may need to expand your circle of advisors. In addition to your financial planner, consider adding an attorney, an accountant or bookkeeper, and perhaps a mentor who can guide you on your quest to create generational wealth. Eventually, every team will need managers who can function as administrators, assistants, bookkeepers, graphic designers, writers, financial analysts, office managers, computer support personnel, technical advisors, sales reps and marketing professionals. In our exercise section write down who you may need on your TEAM (Exercise 7).

Building your team will take time, but remember that you are the leader of this team, the one person who is in charge of the team and who will be in command.

No one person and no one investment will lead directly to your dream. Each person can contribute to fulfilling your goals but ultimately the achievement will be yours.

Key Players on your Team: a Financial Advisor and a Real Estate Professional

The first key player in your team of wealth will be your financial advisor or consultant. This individual will help you with long term wealth management and stocks, bonds and mutual funds. Next, finding a good real estate coach is equally essential. A good real estate coach will work with your financial advisor to create a well-rounded and complete portfolio.

Your financial advisor will assist you with your finances by advising you on investments and providing you with investment opportunities, as well as evaluating your overall financial plan to make sure you are on the right path to meet all your goals. However, financial advisors do not get paid to put you into real estate deals unless it is a publicly traded REIT (Real Estate Investment Trust) so finding a good financial advisor who also understands the value of real estate investing and that there is a time for everything is essential.

All financial markets are cyclical.

When real estate is a good investment, the stock market may be volatile; and when real estate is volatile the stock market is good.

The key element is balance.

Real estate has always been critical to a good financial plan. Have you ever heard of a millionaire who doesn't own a home or even more than one property? However, investing in real estate, as in other types of investing, requires that the buyer beware. **You make money in real estate depending on when and how you buy. You just collect your profit when you sell.** So finding the right real estate professional is a big priority.

A warning: plenty of real estate agents will tell you what you want to hear and proclaim their experience in every facet of the business in order to get YOUR business.

Remember "due diligence?" You can't skip this step. Spend some time researching the agent to discover the truth about their expertise.

One of the best ways to find a reliable agent is to ask colleagues to recommend someone they respect. Another is to find an agent with a consistently strong presence in a neighborhood where you want to purchase property.

Before agreeing to hire an agent to represent you, ask some of these questions:

- What did you do during the down market to adapt your business?
- How many foreclosure or auction transactions did you handle last year? (Ask this question if you intend to invest in foreclosures or buy at an auction)
- Can you provide me with references from your past clients?
- Can you tell me about any financing programs I might qualify for?
- Do you specialize in any particular neighborhoods? Any particular price range?
- How long have you been in business?

In addition to asking questions directly of a potential agent, spend a few minutes online checking to see if the agent is registered with the Better Business Bureau and licensed with your state's Real Estate Commission. Next, simply Google the real estate agent's name to see what comes up about their background.

As you work on your long-term financial goals, don't lose sight of your retirement, and providing a stream of income for your children and grandchildren. Throughout your journey, you may encounter other milestones that require your attention such as buying homes, paying for college tuition, perhaps relocating to further your career and even taking a dream vacation. A good financial advisor can provide you with the planning help required to reach all these milestones. This requires expertise other than just suggesting stocks.

Always remember your financial advisors and consultants make money off your investments. This is why you must be aware of every suggestion and every decision being made about your finances regardless of your choice of financial consultants. Know why certain things are being done with your money.

Because your financial advisor/consultant makes money off your investments, keep in mind that you are the only one who will have your interests as the highest priority. An excellent financial advisor will represent *your* interests, but remember that this is a business for that consultant, not his or her life. This is one reason your choice of consultants is so important. Take your time when interviewing candidates for the job.

Remember this isn't a race to the top but a long journey. Throughout this journey, you will take responsibility for your decisions. You want to surround yourself with the best team members.

Start by gathering recommendations from coworkers, friends, family members, or other trusted professionals with whom you have worked in the past. Realtors and mortgage lenders often have relationships with financial advisors. My business, TEAM Investments, has a small network of trusted financial advisors you may want to interview. Make a list of at least three financial advisors and set up an appointment to meet with each of them to evaluate whether you can build a long-term relationship with this person. Bring a notebook so you can write down responses to your questions. (Exercise 8) Ask for written materials from each potential financial consultant to review once you get home. This way, you can make an unemotional decision when evaluating your choices.

Build Your Team - How to Choose a Financial Advisor or Real Estate Expert:

Initial Meeting with a Financial Advisor or Real Estate Expert

The first meeting with a financial advisor should be like a first date.

Ask questions of one another to see if you are compatible and can continue a progressive relationship. Don't be shy about asking as many questions as you can. Be prepared to ask some questions that might be embarrassing in a social setting, such as, "What are you invested in?" and, "What are you worth?" A good financial advisor will recognize that sharing financial information should be part of building a relationship built on trust.

Be ready to answer some questions, too.

Tell the financial consultant what you expect to gain from the relationship. Explain your goals and tell them how far along you are toward reaching those goals. Clearly expressing your needs and your abilities will allow the consultant to decide if he is capable of helping you achieve your goals.

Once you have moved beyond the initial "first date" questions, it is time to get deeper into evaluating the credentials of your potential financial advisor, including his/her strengths and weaknesses.

Experience

Knowing how long someone has been in business should always be a consideration, whether you are a hiring a doctor or a carpenter.

But experience should not be the determining factor. Someone can have many years of experience, but a bad attitude toward their job. Another person in the same firm can be relatively new, but a real dynamo really working hard to make changes...make a difference. The level of experience can help you assess someone's eligibility to work with you and also serve as a great tool when negotiating a fee. Remember, though, that just because someone has been in business a long time doesn't mean that person is the best one to meet your needs.

For example, Realtors often stress their years of experience when meeting with potential clients. But a new agent can sometimes provide better service because she is eager to prove herself in the business and build a referral base. Experienced agents sometimes have more clients than they can handle. The important aspect of experience is to evaluate how someone's experience translates to meeting your needs. If you are considering working with an inexperienced real estate agent or a relatively new financial advisor, you should ask them about their mentors and whether they have a network of support that they can rely on as they work with you.

Don't be afraid to ask questions.

In addition to finding out the depth of someone's experience, find out the types of clientele they are used to working with. Some financial advisors work mainly with big corporations or small start-up businesses or with individuals with different levels of assets. If you are a novice investor, ready to start on a small level toward building your wealth, you may not want to work with a consultant who mostly spends his time with experienced investors with a portfolio worth millions.

After you have discussed their experience and how it relates to your interests, allow the advisor to explain her approach to you. If you are still learning about investing and financial planning, your best choice of an advisor would be someone willing to spend significant time counseling you and educating you about your choices.

Qualifications

Anyone can say that they are a financial expert. Just saying so, however, doesn't make it so.

Make sure you ask your potential financial consultant about his qualifications. Financial advisors can earn recognition as a Certified Financial Planner, a Certified Personal Financial Specialist or a Certified Public Accountant. Such a certification is a valid recommendation that the individual has extensive knowledge in the field of financial planning. If your potential advisor mentions any type of certification, check her background by contacting the professional organization to which she belongs.

Remember, trust, but verify.

You can also ask your advisor why he feels he is qualified to offer financial advice. Ask him what tools and steps he will use to stay current with the changing market. Keep in mind that an advisor who has proven knowledge in tax, retirement and estate planning as well as insurance and investments will be the most valuable in the long run. The more expansive your advisor's knowledge the more he can pass on to you.

Services

Be sure you discuss exactly what services you will receive from your potential advisor. Find out everything this advisor provides for his clients. Is it advice only in specific areas or an overall financial plan? If the advice is specific, find out exactly which areas will be covered. Is the advisor licensed to sell mutual funds or stocks? In most cases, financial advisors cannot sell insurance or securities without securing the correct license.

Advisors must be registered with the correct association in order to provide investment advice. You are responsible for getting this information from the advisor and validating the information through research. If you are not sure how to go about checking on the advisor's affiliation with an organization, ask the advisor. A reputable financial consultant will provide you with the information you need. If not, then move on to interview the next potential financial consultant. Anyone who is accredited and licensed in their required field will allow you to research those credentials.

Be sure to follow through with this research. Just because someone is accredited does not mean they have always been trustworthy. Make sure they still have that license and that there are not complaints against them. You can check their name against their association, FINRA (Financial Industry Regulatory Authority) and the Better

Business Bureau, or even simply Google the name of the advisor to see what information pops up.

Approach

Everyone has a style, whether it involves their clothing or their approach to work. When it comes to finances, most people have a particular approach to handling money. For some people, that approach involves hiding their head under the pillow and ignoring their finances. Most financial advisors enjoy working with money and developing a strategy that meets the needs of their clients.

Ask your potential advisor what type of financial situation he most enjoys. If he says he prefers working with clients who allow him complete freedom of decision-making, this may be someone you want to avoid. Turning your money over to someone who wants to control it will not give you the ability to lead your wealth. Remember, you must control your money. You're looking for advice here, not a control freak.

At the initial meeting, a potential financial consultant will not be prepared to present your entire financial plan, but you can ask how this advisor would generally approach your specific situation. Ask how she would proceed at the next meeting and how broad or specific she is when it comes to developing a plan.

Ask about his view on investing. Is he aggressive or cautious? See how this approach fits in with yours. Imagine trying to work with a conservative advisor if you are ready to invest aggressively and in an innovative way. While having an advisor with a different view than your own could provide some needed balance to your investment approach, you ought to get the sense that your advisor will listen carefully to your needs.

Ask about financial limits. Some advisors or consultants only work with clients with a specific minimum amount to invest or a maximum.

Ask about the specifics of their approach. If your advisor recommends an opportunity to you, will he follow through and acquire it or will he outsource you to someone else? Listen carefully to his answer and think about how you feel about his approach.

Relationship

Some financial advisors and real estate coaches work independently and will personally handle each customer. Others have assistants or work with a team of consultants. If your advisor or your real estate agent will be sharing your specific financial concerns with other people, make sure you meet those people at an early meeting. Interview each of these assistants or consultants in the same way you interview your main advisor. If the advisor outsources some work to other professionals, make sure you set up meetings with those individuals and research their backgrounds and credentials.

All of this may seem like an excessive amount of caution, but when you consider the importance of the relationship between you and your advisors, it makes sense to take a lot of time choosing the right people. You must feel comfortable with your advisors and your advisors' associates in order to be in control of your finances.

You may find that you are comfortable with your advisor but not with someone on your advisor's team or, during the course of your research, you may find that your advisor is outsourcing work to someone who isn't reputable enough for you. If this happens, ask your potential advisor if she would be willing to work with someone else. Perhaps you can even recommend someone else and provide references. If they are willing to work with someone you recommend, this can be a sign that you have found a good consultant. If not, you may want to move on.

The most important person in this process is you. You must be confident that you are creating a team of trustworthy advisors who will follow your lead and help you reach your goals.

Compensation

An important consideration in your choice of a financial advisor should be the method of payment. This should be discussed at your initial meeting and will be included in the written agreement you and your final choice of advisor will sign.

When you are working with a financial advisor who is selling you stocks, as many as seven people can sometimes be paid before you see the profits from your investment.

In real estate investing, first you will pay a commission to a real estate agent who lists and sells your property, then you be directly paid for the sale of the property. Real estate commissions are negotiable and if you develop a long-term relationship with an agent who will represent you in multiple transactions you may be able to spend less on commission payments than you would if you work with several real estate professionals. In real estate, the line from your investment directly to your bank account is much shorter than in other types of investments.

Some financial advisors are paid by their company, which usually means you are paying a fee or commission to that company and then the company pays a salary to your advisor. Other financial consultants have an hourly rate, a set fee, or even get paid as a percentage of your assets. Some advisors are paid by a commission from the product they sell you, which is calculated by taking a percentage of the amount of money you invest. If this is how the advisor is paid, ask what percentage you will be required to pay.

Take note of this percentage if you choose to work with an advisor paid by commission and keep an eye on the recommendations of this advisor. Some advisors may allow their opinion to be influenced regarding a particular investment opportunity if this will increase their commission. They may recommend a product that works well for them (by increasing their pay) but not for you. Always be cautious about why anyone is recommending something to you. Ask for a detailed explanation of why something is recommended and then do your own research before coming to a conclusion.

Some advisors are paid through a combination of a set fee and a commission. They may charge a flat fee for consultation and then subtract a commission from any investment you make.

The pay structure may influence the types of investments an advisor suggests. For example, many financial consultants don't include real estate in their client's portfolio because they are not paid a commission to recommend real estate. A financial advisor paid by commission through stock investments can still be of value to you, but make sure you understand the ramifications of working with someone who will not always be considering your broader financial needs. Make sure you evaluate the possibilities of investing in real estate on your own or consult with a real estate expert in your area so that you don't neglect this potentially lucrative investment.

Evaluating a pay structure can be complicated. Rely on your research and understanding of how your potential financial advisor works.

Always remember that you are in control of your wealth. Never feel pressured to purchase or invest in anything you are not comfortable with or anything on which you have not done your due diligence.

Negotiations

Often financial advisors won't be able to give you an exact price for their services, especially when they work based on commissions. After you have had a general discussion of your assets and your financial plans, an advisor should be able to give you an estimate of what you can expect to pay for their services.

Remember, an estimate is exactly that, an estimate. It isn't something you can hold your advisor to in the future.

When you receive an estimate rather than a standard fee structure, you may be able to negotiate with the potential advisor. If the advisor lacks experience, yet you still are comfortable with their knowledge and ability to handle your money, you might be able to negotiate a lower price.

If you are working with someone with a proven track record, you are less likely to be able to lower their fee.

Estimates of the fees for a financial advisor should be used to determine your ultimate profit. If you feel that your potential profits will be seriously undermined by fees, continue searching for an advisor who is more affordable. But be careful. While there are times when you can find someone willing to lower their fees, make sure that advisor still has the knowledge and skills you need.

Don't short yourself in the long run by opting for a cheaper alternative.

Ethics

While most professions have a standard of ethics that applies to every individual working in that field, financial advisors work in a field with myriad temptations for unethical behavior. Not only do advisors have access to detailed financial information about their clients, but they are constantly encouraged to sell particular services or products by outside companies.

This combination of pressures makes this a field that requires extremely strong ethics.

Realtors, who must be members of the National Association of Realtors in order to use that title, can be disciplined by their Association if they do not adhere to their strict Code of Ethics. While real estate transactions require written contracts signed by the buyers, the sellers and their representatives, there are still plenty of opportunities for agents to behave unethically in order to keep more money for themselves.

You may feel awkward, but ask your potential financial consultant and your real estate agent if she has ever been disciplined for unethical behavior.

In addition to listening carefully to her response, follow up by checking with your state board of insurance and securities departments and the state real estate commission to research disciplinary action. You can also check with the National Association of Securities Dealers.

The Financial Industry Regulatory Authority (FINRA) has a free online tool known as Broker Check that allows consumers to check the licensing information and disciplinary action of any investment advisor:

finra.org/Investors/ToolsCalculators/BrokerCheck/index.htm

The Securities and Exchange Commission (Sec.gov) uses a form called Form ADV for an advisor registration that includes a section on disciplinary action. You can request a copy of this form from your potential advisor and also check the form online at the SEC.

Agreement

Throughout the chapter on making wise decisions, we emphasized the importance of writing down your thoughts and your research.

When it comes to choosing a financial advisor and a real estate agent, getting everything in writing becomes even more valuable.

Ask your potential advisors to give you everything they can in writing, including a description of services and fees. Keep this information as a reference when making your decision and after you have chosen an advisor or a real estate agent.

In most states, real estate agents will be required to sign a buyer-agent agreement or a listing agent-seller agreement that will clearly establish their responsibilities and yours. Pay careful attention to how the agreement can be dissolved if either party is unhappy with the relationship. While you are doing your best to choose the right real estate agent, sometimes a home seller or buyer finds that the agent is not fulfilling their expectations. In this case, be sure you understand what you must do to end the agreement.

When you receive written agreements from each advisor you interview, compare their fees and services to evaluate which matches your needs. You can even use this comparison as a method for negotiating fees. If one advisor charges less for one service than another or a different consultant performs more services for the same amount of money, you can use this information to create your own contract to present as an offer to your advisor of choice.

In the world of finance everything is negotiable.

If you present a reasonable offer with solid research to back up your offer, there could be room for change. Just be sure your offer is truly reasonable. A request for an extremely low level of compensation could be insulting to an experienced financial advisor or real estate agent and ruin a relationship that you have just begun to cultivate.

The negotiating process, along with the time spent in interviews, should help you get to know your potential advisor better. You may not want an advisor who will talk down to you and act like a teacher at all times – after all, you are the one in control and you are asking for advice, not a lecture. However, a willingness to explain what he recommends and why he recommends it should be a valuable trait in any financial consultant or real estate agent. If you are selling a home, you may find yourself insulted by a real estate agent who is critical of your property. Try to remember that this agent is an expert in recognizing what buyers want and can help you sell the residence or commercial property for the highest possible price. Keep your emotions out of your business dealings.

Choosing a Financial Advisor and Real Estate Expert

As you meet with each potential advisor and real estate expert you will request printed information from them about their services and save this with the notes you have taken during your interviews. If you are not satisfied with the initial group of financial consultants you have met on your "first dates", then date some more.

Remember, choosing a financial consultant or real estate agent may be similar to searching for a spouse, but if you have made a bad decision it is a lot easier to move on to the next consultant than to get a divorce.

Making a wise decision on a financial advisor and a real estate professional requires the same steps as any other decision.

Pull out your notes to remind yourself of your meeting with each advisor. Think about how you felt about the meeting and whether you were comfortable with the consultant or real estate agent. Did you feel as if you could establish a relationship with her? Did you feel he was listening to you and your needs and was genuinely interested in helping you achieve your goals? Or did you think she was trying to sell you something you don't want or need?

Take as much time as necessary to think about the financial advisors and real estate professionals you met.

Sleep on it.

Remember that you are about to develop a long-term relationship. You must be able to trust your advisors and feel confident that your advisors will listen to you.

A financial advisor and a real estate expert can be valuable, but remember you are not obligated to hire one. Keep in mind that the key element of the term financial advisor is the word "advisor".

You are the *decision-maker*.

Never rely entirely on one person other than yourself to make decisions involving your money. Remain in control of your money at all times.

Moving Ahead With Your Team in Place
Working with Your Team

Whether you have found them individually or they work together as a team, be ready to consult with your accountants, lawyers, mentors, real estate experts and financial advisors. Once you have developed this team you must respect their opinions and consider their expertise. Always keep the lines of communication open with every member of your team.

Communication and respect do not necessarily mean, however, that you must follow every recommendation blindly. The reason you have carefully assembled this team is so that you can access their knowledge and then make your own judgment.

If a recommendation comes from an advisor or real estate agent and you feel uncertain about it, take the time to think about it. Read up on the topic, ask the opinion of other experts and draw your own conclusion. The investment opportunity will be there when you are ready, so never feel pressured into a quick decision just because someone else has promoted it. If the opportunity has disappeared by the time you decide, then maybe that was not the right opportunity for you.

It is always better to be able to rest knowing you made a measured, wise decision rather than rushing to become involved in something that will leave you worried. Take your time. It took time to create the money you now have available to invest. Don't throw it away on something you have doubts about.

Always resolve to know everything that is going on with your finances. Seek out new ventures and create new ways of making money. Leave room for additional advisors and mentors. Nothing should be static when it comes to growing your money.

Overcoming Doubt

By applying the lessons you learned in making wise decisions and choosing advisors and members of your team your self-confidence will grow. A person who knows how to make wise decisions should have self-confidence, right?

But in reality, every single person has some doubt inside themselves about their ability to achieve their goals. Conquering your fear can be the ultimate confidence-builder, allowing you to soar above even your highest expectations.

Fear may be too strong a word for something that stops plenty of people in their tracks. It might be better described as "discomfort with stepping outside their safety zone." Individuals who never move past surrounding themselves with people they feel most comfortable to be around, working at a job they know how to do, or visiting only places where they have been before may live a serene life, but they will never experience that empowering moment when they triumph over that inner voice that keeps saying "you can't."

Doubt is the number one enemy of success.

It stops people from capitalizing on opportunities. It stops them from dreaming big and acting on that dream. Think about the physical manifestation of fear: your heart beats faster, you either run away or you stand stock still in your tracks. Have you ever had a moment or two of panic and then noticed how exhausted you feel when the terror fades? Fear breaks down your physical and your emotional vitality.

Conquering anxiety is never easy, yet plenty of people manage to move beyond their doubts every day to find solutions to their problems and to live beyond their own expectations. Believing a solution to your problems is possible paves the way to finding that solution.

Start by eliminating the words "can't", "won't", "never happen" from your vocabulary and replace these words with positive phrases such as "I can", "I will", "I can do this" and "I will make this happen."

Be progressive in everything you do.

Ask yourself every day if there is something you can do better. There is no limit to self-improvement. Plenty of people suffer from a fear of public speaking. Some will simply arrange their lives so they never have to make a presentation in front of a group. Others determine that conquering this anxiety can lead to success in their careers or even to a change of a career path into something more rewarding. By taking a stand, forcing themselves out of their comfort zone, preparing a presentation and then speaking to a group, individuals can build their confidence in countless ways.

Every day, try to ask yourself if you can do more with your life, with your time. You may feel that you don't have enough time to educate yourself about investing and building wealth, but take the time to evaluate your long-term goals. If one of your goals is to build generational wealth, then nothing sill stop you from finding the time to overcome your fear about your lack of knowledge or your concern about taking risks.

Keep track of how you spend your time for a few days to see where you can create the time to do more.

Capacity is a state of mind. Managing your time requires a strong sense of discipline and a budget for your time just like the one you ought to have for your money.

Leading Your Circle

You will learn more in the next chapter how to run your life like a business and keep your finances in order.

For now, focus on strengthening your connections with your financial team.

Make it a habit to stay in constant communication with your advisors and real estate experts. Schedule quarterly, semi-annual, or annual meetings to review where you were and where you are now, and how you are going to continue to reach your goals. (Exercise 9)

Begin developing the habit of reading magazines, newspaper articles and books about investing and creating wealth and share what you learn with your advisors. As your confidence and your profits grow, you may find yourself more willing to take risks. Just remember to take the steps to make a wise decision each time you are ready to invest in a new venture.

Keep your team of mentors and advisors close at hand and always be the leader rather than the follower. You are the commander in chief with a trusted team of advisors.

Remember you are the ultimate boss and decision maker.

PRINCIPLE THREE - RUN YOUR LIFE
LIKE A BUSINESS

Every profitable business relies on a balance sheet. Even non-profit organizations use a budget so that, at a glance, staff and directors can view an accurate picture of the company cash flow. Yet plenty of Americans operate without the slightest idea of how much they are spending and where their money goes. The average American has nineteen credit card and loan accounts open at any one time. No wonder so many people struggle to meet their monthly obligations.

With the recent financial crisis our global economy has been through the average savings rate is in the negative numbers, meaning that consumers are adding more debt to their balance sheet than savings every single month.

If you recognize yourself among those people who don't have money in the bank for emergencies, who don't know where their money goes each day or each month, then it's time to treat your own life as if you were a business. No matter how motivated you are, your financial goals cannot be met until you recognize the necessity of balancing your books.

We have talked about the importance of making wise decisions, establishing your values and setting goals. In this chapter we will begin the practical application of these steps to your finances.

Once you have rid yourself of your negative views about money and are prepared to adjust your decision-making in accordance with your goals, it is time to begin watering the seeds of your money tree.

Start by recognizing the misconception that money is scarce and your limited funds are what prevent you from achieving financial freedom. It is the absence of willpower to gain control of spending and to develop new sources of income that keep people from meeting their financial goals.

Most people want a better financial future for themselves and their families, but they also think they are too far in debt or don't have the ability to make enough money to change their pattern. In order to build wealth take the struggle out of earning money and turn it into a challenge. No one but you can understand the difference in your attitude when you switch off the negativity of the word "struggle" and replace it with the positive word "challenge." Not every challenge is fun, of course, but most people find challenge motivating. Instead of struggling to climb a mountain, you are setting higher and higher goals and encouraging yourself by meeting each one.

It is time to put into practice your ability to make wise decisions about your money.

Controlling your Cash Flow

For most people, budgeting has a negative connotation. Budgeting your money feels like you are focusing solely on what you cannot do instead of what you can do. Instead, set a goal of knowing exactly how much you are spending each month. You will never find a successful business that is not using a budget. (Exercise 10) They spend months on end planning the year's budget and planning how to adhere to it. You must do the same.

Reviewing your spending patterns and being conscious of your spending choices stops you from frivolous expenditures. It doesn't mean that you can no longer buy things that give you pleasure or take vacations or dine out in a fancy restaurant. You must simply recognize that while you have every right to spend your money any way you choose, you must also learn how to create ways to make more money.

The key to financial abundance is to have a constant flow of money sweeping in and out of your life. If you are spending too much money then your well of finances will dry up, putting you back into a state of financial stress.

Money takes both responsibility and activity. Budgeting fulfills the responsibility side of this equation, but using your money wisely expands your financial strength by demanding both responsible spending and actions to create wealth.

Developing a business plan for your life isn't about budgeting or about penny pinching. It's about creating opportunities for money to flow into your life.

Understanding the Role of Debt

Many people assume that all debt is bad and that every debt should be avoided at all costs or at least paid off in full as soon as possible. This is a common misperception.

There are two types of debt: good debt and bad debt. Being able to differentiate between the two is a sign of someone who is sophisticated in their understanding of money.

Bad debt or consumer debt is the debt you acquired to buy things that will eventually lose value. There is no obvious benefit to your finances in bad debt.

Good debt is debt used to buy things that will increase in value over time.

Both types of debt have a role to play in your plans for creating wealth. (Exercise 11) First, it is imperative to do away with bad debt. Bad debt only takes away from your supply of money for spending and investing. Worry about bad debt creates stress and distracts your focus from your goals.

Good debt can help you reach your goals by creating opportunities to make more money.

Handling Good Debt

While having an unlimited supply of funds for investing and making major purchases would be lovely, we must recognize that few people have that type of wealth. Instead, most people need to borrow money for items that will eventually generate more wealth. Real estate loans for investment properties or for your principal residence can be beneficial to individuals who want to create wealth by owning property that will increase in value over time. With the recent turn in the real estate market it is imperative to have a good professional telling you when to buy and when to sell or the good debt you are accumulating can turn into bad debt very quickly. Business loans are also sources of good debt, necessary for most entrepreneurs before they generate a steady stream of income.

Many people share the goal of owning their home mortgage-free. One step on the path to owning property free-and-clear of debt is to refinance your current mortgage. Some homeowners refinance to a shorter loan term as their income rises and try to correlate their mortgage pay-off date with their retirement.

Refinancing a home loan can also be used to reduce your spending on interest payments. This can save you $100 or more on a monthly basis and thousands over the life of the mortgage. In addition to creating additional cash flow each month, refinancing can be used to generate cash for making home improvements that will quickly add value to your property.

Home loans can function as good debt in two ways: first, the mortgage is being used to purchase something that should increase in value over time, unlike using a credit card to buy a meal, which will have no value by the time your bill is paid. Second, as you pay down your mortgage you are not only paying off the debt but with each payment you shift the balance of your debt to the value of the property. Rent payments provide individuals with a place to live but do nothing to build their portfolio of assets.

Good debt allows your money to work for you. If you are considering whether to go into debt for anything, make sure you use your wise decision-making skills to weight the benefits of borrowing. If you will eventually get back more than what you borrowed, this is a signal that this could be good debt.

Bad Debt

The opposite is true of bad debt. If you borrow money to buy something that instantly loses its value, then there is no benefit to that debt. If your purchase has no promise of increasing in value the way real estate or an investment or a business does, then this is not a purchase to make by using debt.

Many people find themselves in debt because of their desire for material possessions such as the newest car or the latest fashion. There's nothing inherently wrong in wanting a new car or a designer dress, but spending money on these and similar items is only acceptable once you have generated the flow of income to sustain your lifestyle.

Studies have shown that most people spend far more money, even at the grocery store, when they use a credit card rather than cash. People often overlook the impact of making purchases with a credit card. When you use a credit card to buy something and you are not prepared to pay the balance in full before the due date, you are automatically increasing the cost of that purchase. Even if you bought something on sale, thinking you were being responsible in buying the item before the price went up, you could end up paying double or triple the original price by the time you add up the interest you will pay by spreading out the purchase over time. Plenty of consumers are tricked by department store promises of 10% off your initial purchase when you accept a new credit card. It's not a trick if you pay the purchase in full before the due date on the credit card. But if you only make the minimum payment on your credit card each month, the department store will get back that 10% and more from your interest payments depending on how long it takes you to pay off the total balance.

Bad debt can be tricky for people who have a handle on their finances and are managing to pay all their bills on time. You may think that because you are not being charged late fees and because you pay the minimum due each month, or even a little more than the minimum, that you are in good shape financially. But if you take the time to total the interest being added to the balance on each of your bad debts every month you will see how costly this borrowing can be. While the credit card companies are happiest with customers who pay on time and only pay the minimum, those are the customers who are simply wasting their money and allowing someone else to benefit from their earnings.

When Should You Borrow Money?

Typically the two major purchases for which people borrow money is for a car and a home. An auto loan would normally be considered bad debt since cars depreciate in value as soon as they are driven off the lot. Yet, given the huge expenditure that new cars require, it may be better to borrow money for the car and allow your savings to be used for other investments. Ideally, it is best to pay cash for a car or at least be managing your money so well that the car dealer offers you extremely low interest financing.

The best type of debt is a mortgage, because paying for property not only gives you a place to live but also grows in value. If you can borrow money for a home before you purchase a car, that would be best, but most people need a car to get to work.

If you have to buy a car before you buy a home, at least try to restrain yourself from buying the most expensive car on the lot. Choosing an affordable car eases your cash flow so that you can afford to spend more on a home.

Debt Management

Carrying a heavy debt load adds stress and worry to your life and can harm your credit rating, which could, in turn, limit your ability to borrow money for good debt. If you miss a payment or are more than thirty days late, your creditors will report this negative information to the credit bureaus. Even if you always pay on time, your credit rating can drop if you have high balances on your credit cards in relation to the credit limit. Negative reports on your credit have a huge impact on your creditability and your score. Tightened standards of credit mean that only individuals with the highest credit scores, at least above 700, will be able to borrow money at the lowest interest rates.

When deciding whether or not to take on new debt, it is important to consider your debt-to-income ratio. This ratio is the percentage of your gross monthly income that goes toward paying your debts. The key to financial independence is to keep this number as low as possible. A good rule of thumb is not to have your personal debt exceed an estimated 36% of your income. Mortgage lenders typically allow borrowers a range of total debt, including all housing payments, up to a maximum of 45%, but financial planners say this level of debt won't allow you enough money for savings and for regular monthly expenses.

When you are working toward your goal of creating wealth you do not want any money to have to go to unnecessary debt. If you want something or need something that will not increase in value then pay cash. If you can't pay cash then don't buy it or wait until you have saved enough cash so you can afford the purchase.

Credit cards should only be used in the case of an emergency such as a car repair or a medical bill. Ideally, you will have saved an emergency fund with cash to pay for such unexpected expenses. If you find yourself having to use your credit card often, then slow down your spending and take the time to create a plan to bring your balance back to zero. Put your credit card in a drawer or a safe place where you won't be tempted to use it. Some people who struggle to curtail their spending opt to store their credit card in the freezer where it would need to be thawed before use. Don't cancel the credit card altogether because this will drop your credit score. One factor that determines your credit score is your overall use of all your available credit. If you cancel a credit card your available credit immediately drops by the credit limit on that card.

Incessant spending must be controlled and is the number one form of mismanaging your money. While some people find themselves deeply in debt because of a divorce, job loss or medical expenses, most people are in debt simply because they spend more money than they save or invest.

Harmful Methods of Debt Reduction

In general, it is always wise to reduce your bad debt. But not all ways of getting out of debt are in your best interest. In fact, some methods can slow your ability to create wealth.

- Bankruptcy. Bankruptcy may sound like the easiest, fastest way to get out of debt because once bankruptcy is declared many of your debts are erased. However, this is a moment when to carefully assess your options and use your wise decision-making skills. Think about the long-term impact of a bankruptcy. Filing for bankruptcy remains on your credit history for at least seven years and will hinder your ability to borrow money in the future. Many employers today are reviewing the credit history of job candidates. A bankruptcy could be viewed as a signal that you are unreliable, irresponsible and unable to handle your finances, which could cost you a job.

  Now that you have decided to create financial abundance you may be in a hurry to eliminate your debt and move on with your plans. Remember to look at the long-term effect of your decisions rather choosing instant gratification. Making wise financial decisions will lead you to a time when you are able to pay your debts in full and take advantage of opportunities without the negative impact of a bankruptcy on your record. Consult an attorney, someone you have researched well and can trust, if you feel that a bankruptcy is your only option. A trustworthy attorney can work with you to make a considered recommendation on whether taking this drastic step is necessary for your specific financial situation.

- Debt Consolidation Companies. If you have ever entered the search term "debt consolidation" on the Internet you have likely been inundated with offers from companies to work with you to reduce your debt. Beware. A lot of these companies will put you on a program in which they total the sum of your debts and arrange an affordable monthly payment. The problem is that this affordable payment is actually only covering the interest on your debts and won't make a dent in the principal balance owed.

Non-profit credit counseling organizations that are certified by the federal government can also work with you to consolidate your debt and may negotiate with your creditors to reduce your interest rate or the balance owed. However, consolidating your debt in this manner will be reported to credit bureaus and could damage your credit rating, in particular if you pay your creditors less than the full amount you owe. If you choose to meet with a credit counselor make sure you ask about the long-term consequences of any action you take.

Another option is to contact your creditors on your own to negotiate a repayment plan that eliminates your late fees, lowers the remaining balance and/or reduces your interest rate. Some creditors will be more willing to work with you than others. Consumers should be aware of two negative consequences of taking this approach in spite of the positive outcome of debt reduction. First, the creditors will report you to the credit bureaus as having "paid less than owed." This will reduce your credit score and remain on your credit report for seven years. Second, the gap between what you pay and what you originally owed will be considered income so you will be responsible for paying federal taxes on the amount.

- Credit Repair Companies. There are some reputable companies that can help you repair your credit but there are an equal or perhaps greater number of credit repair companies who rely on illegal methods of removing negative items from your credit history. Before opting to work with a credit repair company, start by getting your own free credit report from all three credit reporting bureaus at AnnualCreditReport.com. When you receive each report, carefully review it for errors. Each agency has a method that to follow to correct mistakes. Make sure you keep a careful record of every step you take to fix errors, including copies of all emails and written materials. Personally correcting errors can be time-consuming but will also give you the satisfaction of knowing the work has been done right and by you.

If your credit history shows negative information that is true, you cannot legally remove it. However, if the time limit for keeping certain information on your report has passed, then you can request for this to be removed. Otherwise, focus on ways to improve your credit report. The website MyFico.com provides plenty of suggestions on steps you can take and choices to make that will have a positive impact on your credit score.

- Transferring your Balances. Some consumers opt to transfer the balance from a high interest credit card to one with a lower interest rate to save money. Many credit card companies offer a teaser rate for new customers that encourage them to transfer the balance from one company to another. Transferring your balance is profitable only if done carefully and correctly. It's one thing to use a low interest rate card to pay off a high interest rate balance once or twice, but it isn't wise to turn this into a cycle. Once you have transferred the balance from the high interest card to the lower interest card don't begin using the high interest card again and run up your balance. This only creates a pattern of continuous high debt and instability and will do nothing to reduce your overall debt. Don't forget to keep the original credit card account open even though you won't use that credit. Closing the account reduces your credit score.

- Refinancing. Some homeowners choose to refinance their home to consolidate their personal debt. This can yield great results because mortgage loans typically have a much lower interest rate than credit cards. In addition, the interest paid on a mortgage loan is usually tax deductible. However, there is a huge danger in refinancing to pay off debt.

Many people who are unable to control their spending transfer their debt to their home, thus reducing the equity they have in the property, and then immediately begin incurring more debt. If you choose to refinance your home to pay off your other debts, make sure you are ready to be responsible about your spending. Don't waste the equity in your home by creating more debt. Remember, too, that if you cannot make the payments on your mortgage you could lose your home. Make sure you are not getting over your head in terms of your mortgage payments.

Getting out of Debt

Feeling guilty over debt won't help you resolve your situation. Remember that you have resolved to eliminate your negative feelings about money. Focus on the positive. Recognize that getting out of debt takes a lot longer than getting into debt.

Reducing your debt requires discipline, dedication and focus. But you can do it. Think about the possibilities you can create for building your wealth once your finances are no longer dragged down by your debt.

Once you develop your plan to get out of debt, you will need to stick to the plan or find yourself repeating an endless cycle of dealing with unwanted bills. Getting out of debt is an important step to running your life like a business. One of the first steps for any successful business owner is to dissolve all bad debts. Think about a restaurant owner for a moment. Obviously an attractive restaurant will require tables, comfortable chairs and a few decorative items. A restaurant owner without a lot of fiscal discipline might go overboard in buying paintings from a favorite artist or expensive curtains or crystal chandeliers. As soon as the restaurant opens, though, the owner will recognize the folly of overspending on non-essential items and begin to reduce the debt incurred by frivolous purchases.

Your Debt Elimination Plan

Now that you have made the wise decision to eliminate your bad debt, it is time to develop a sound plan that will move your forward to your ultimate goal of building wealth.

1. **List your debts**. Make a list of every single creditor you have, with a column for the total balance owed, the minimum monthly payment and the interest rate.

2. **Prioritize your debts.** Take a moment to catch your breath. Many people find themselves surprised by the amount of money they owe when they create this list. Hopefully, you will be pleasantly surprised that you owe less than you thought. If not, just reaffirm your ability to work through the steps of debt reduction and become financially free. Now, reorganize your list of debts. Put the debt with the highest interest rate first and then list each additional debt in order from highest to lowest interest rate. This is the order in which you will pay off your debts. Visualize your relief when you reach that debt on the bottom line. When you pay off that balance you will be free of the stress of debt payments.

3. **Set aside a specific payment amount**. Now that you are in control of the order in which you intend to pay off your debts, set aside a specific amount that you

will pay each bill every month. In order to make significant progress toward reducing and eventually eliminating the balance on that first debt, you will need to pay much more than the minimum payment. Make sure you have enough income to pay the minimum amount due on all other bills, and then devote as much money as possible to paying off the balance on your highest interest debt. Aim to pay at least double the minimum payment or more if you can manage it. The more you can pay toward that one debt, the faster you will find yourself eliminating all your debts.

4. **Payments.** As you are devoting as much money as possible to reducing the balance on debt number one, make sure you continue to make the minimum payments on all your other debts. Next, once you have paid the first debt in full, you will need to call on your strength and discipline to take the amount of money you were spending on that bill and apply it to the next bill on your list. For example, if you paid $250 each month on debt number one and it is now paid in full; don't assume you now have an extra $250 per month to spend on fun. Nope. Now you must add $250 to the payment you were already making (the minimum payment, presumably) to the second debt on your list. The fun doesn't start when debt number two is paid off, either. At that point, add the entire payment you were making on that debt together with the minimum payment on debt number three to pay that creditor. For example, if you were paying $50 per month on debt number two, you

would have paid that debt at a rate of $300 per month. When you reach the third debt on your list, you will be paying $300 per month on that one plus the minimum payment you were already making. By now, your debt reduction plan should be showing significant progress. Your cash flow situation won't have changed, but if you will have reduced your overall debt and should begin to see the possibility of becoming debt free. Pull out your list of creditors as each debt is paid off and total again the remaining balances due and the minimum monthly payments required so you can track your progress.

5. **Meeting your Obligations.** I am sure you would never deliberately choose not to pay your utility bill or make a payment to your child's day-care provider. You must view your debt repayment plan as the same level of obligation as these bills. It will be tempting to fall back and choose to return to making only the minimum payments on your credit card bills because, after all, that will mean you have more money available for spending. Keep your focus on your long-term goals and be proud of your progressive toward becoming debt free. Make the commitment to stick to your plan, even when it seems crazy to send so much money to a creditor who would be satisfied with less. Many people find that as they continue to pay off their balances they want to pay more and more to their creditors so they can get out of debt faster. The vision of the liberating moment of being debt free should remain in your mind every time you pay a bill. Keep reminding yourself of the possibilities that will

open to you when you no longer have debt obligations to pay. Remember that even though you have set up a plan for eliminating your debt, your plan is adjustable. Always be looking for extra money that you can apply to reducing your debt. If you have the time or the ability to earn extra money at a temporary job to increase the income you can use to pay bills, consider giving up some leisure time to reach your ultimate goal of creating wealth. The faster you get out of debt the more quickly you can move toward achieving financial abundance.

Moving Beyond Debt

Now that you have begun the process of eliminating your debt and have developed a vision of your future financial abundance, it is time to a detailed look at your spending and expenses. There is simply no other way to accurately evaluate whether you are making your money work for you.

In order to map your route to reaching your financial goals, take a realistic look at where you are now and where you would like to be. Once again, it is crucial to put everything on paper. Months or years from now as reap the joy of your financial success you will want to be able to track your path. It would be impossible to know how far you have come if you don't have documentation of where you started. Be honest and detailed in your written materials.

Make sure you include every amount of money you bring into your life and every single expense you have, along with everything you own and everything you owe.

Details count. If you leave something out you will not have an accurate image of your current situation.

Look back at Exercise 2 as your base.

This is where you begin to see how your life works like a business. You may become fearful or frustrated when you reduce your finances to a single chart. Some people judge themselves and turn their negative feelings into a lack of motivation.

You have already faced up to your debt and understand how to make wise decisions, so don't let any disappointment in your finances deter you from improving them. Your current financial picture isn't the real concern. Always be thinking about where you are going, not where you are now.

Now that you have your base, the next project is to develop your detailed list of goals. Include anything from the smallest achievement you wish to accomplish, such as paying off one credit card, to your biggest dreams, such as owning a home, gathering a specific amount of money for savings, earning a specific return on your investments, creating a trust fund for a child or taking a trip around the world.

Your list of goals can be as short or as long as you wish, but be realistic, too. Don't just write down "I want ten million dollars in the bank by next year", if you are currently deeply in debt. Instead, start with some goals you can meet before moving to some pie-in-the-sky desire.

Go back and look at Exercise 2, now create it again with how you want it to look and use this for your goals.

Timing

All goals should come with a timeframe. Otherwise, you are simply writing down wishes instead of concrete objectives. Do allow yourself a reasonable amount of time to reach your targets.

Ideally, you could set a three-month timeframe for getting your life in order to head toward your goals. Then allow yourself at least one year to accomplish some of your aspirations.

If you create a plan that will give you some results immediately, this will help you stay motivated. The more realistic your plan and your timeframe, the less likely you are to become disappointed and turn away from your dreams.

Creating the Flow

Now that you understand your base, have your list of goals and a timeframe in place, it is time to move forward and develop a flow that will continually feed into your plan. You are ready to create a plan for how you are going to control your money in a way that will allow you to accomplish your goals. This plan includes two elements: how you are going to spend your money and how you can create a continuous flow of more money coming in and less money going out.

First, keep a monthly chart of how much you are spending and where your money goes. Again, your honesty here is crucial. If you are denying the truth about your spending you cannot gain control of your money.

Every month write down everything you bought, every amount you donated to your church or temple or to charity, and every bill you paid. A great tool to use that will help you with maintain accuracy is to keep all receipts. Or pay for everything with a debit card (NOT a credit card, it is too tempting not to pay the balance in full) so that each item will appear on your bank statement.

If you are disciplined enough to pay off your credit card balance in full every month, get a credit card with rewards would be a great option. You can earn rewards such as airline miles, hotel rooms, gift cards or even cash-back while receiving a monthly statement that details your spending.

Other options for tracking spending include software programs for your computer or applications for your iPhone or Android. Of course, these programs still require you to be vigilant about entering every penny you spend.

There are so many options for tracking your spending that it should be simple to choose one that matches your lifestyle. Once you have your spending habits written before you, it will be easier to readjust them to make sure you are headed in the right direction of controlling the flow of money.

Writing down your spending is only the beginning of the process of creating an increasing flow of money into your life rather than out. Dissect the amount you are spending in each category. This may be the moment when you find a software program (such as Quicken or Microsoft Money) that will automatically create charts and graphs of your spending.

Set aside some time at the end of your first month of tracking spending, perhaps with a cup of tea or a glass of wine so you will feel relaxed and ready to start making some considered decisions.

Look over your spending list.

Does any particular amount strike you as too big? Expect your rent or mortgage payment to be the largest, but any other total that looks larger than you anticipated should be studied. This is a red flag of overspending. Once you find an area like this (dining out, shoe shopping, too-frequent happy hour evenings with friends), see if you can find a way to cut down spending in that area. For example, consider hosting an occasional pot-luck dinner or inexpensive pizza party rather than always going out. Shop your closet instead of your local mall. You may be surprised at how many clothing items or pairs of shoes are hidden in the back corner of your closet. Use your money-spending chart to see how much money you can actually save by cutting back in several areas.

Keeping track of your spending is a tried-and-true method of money management. It is a valuable tool that allows you to see where you are wasting money. Once you recognize that you are spending a shocking $100 or more each month on take-out coffee, you will be more willing to move toward better spending habits. This does not mean you have to stop buying coffee every day; better spending habits simply means setting your priorities. If you need to reduce your spending in order to have more money to invest, you can decide that a daily coffee is too important to your sense of well-being or your routines to give up. You are in control. You can choose another place to reduce your spending.

Everyone needs to develop a healthy relationship with money, to view it as a path to freedom. Once you recognize that frivolous spending habits are a hindrance to reaching your objective of financial abundance, you will begin to respect your money more and become increasingly cautious in your spending.

As you continue to pay attention to your spending you are likely to realize that you have extra money each month. Put this money into a separate account that you will use first for debt elimination and later towards investments. A money market account is a good option for this cash since you will earn interest on the money. However, money market accounts are limited to six free withdrawals per month, so be sure that you won't be accessing the money more often than that. While you are using the money for debt elimination, you can transfer a lump sum to your regular checking account once each month to pay several bills if necessary.

Continue keeping track of your money each month, even after you have accomplished your goals. Find a place to write in big bold letters "REMEMBER TO CHART YOUR SPENDING." If you have a bulletin board in your office or keep reminders on your refrigerator door or refer often to a calendar, place those five words where you will see them as often as possible.

Without maintaining vigilance you may find it easy to slip back into overspending. Once you find the method that is easiest for you and get into the habit of watching your spending, you will find the process less time-consuming than it will be during the first few months. The good thing about whichever method you use to track your spending is that nothing must be written in stone – you can constantly adjust your spending or even the way you track it. As your finances improve and your income grows you can adjust your spending accordingly.

Transforming your Life into a Business

Now that you have begun to translate your personal finances into an organized, businesslike system, your next step is to truly become a business by creating an entity. An entity can range from a limited liability corporation (LLC) to a partnership or a corporation. The first purpose of creating an entity is for the protection of your assets. The second purpose is to ignite the spark of an entrepreneurial spirit. You can have the experience of running a business along with the opportunity to make more money doing what you enjoy.

Another important reason for creating an entity and allocating your money into a business is the tax advantage. There are two tax systems in the United States. In the first system, people make money, pay taxes on their earnings and then spend the remainder. This is the system used by uneducated taxpayers.

Knowledgeable taxpayers use a more profitable approach. With this system, individuals can make money, spend money and then pay taxes on the remainder. Most Americans make money, pay taxes, and then spend what is left over, by flipping those final two steps; individuals can greatly reduce their tax liability. The majority of Americans are overpaying on taxes because of their lack of knowledge of how to organize their finances and run their lives like a business.

Restructuring your Taxes

The more organized your finances are, the easier it will be to utilize the tax strategies that allow you to keep more of your earnings. You will need to create a business venture that brings in revenue and allows you to write off a wide range of expenses.

A wide range of options are available for business ventures. Take the time to evaluate your situation to decide which entity meets your needs.

Consult with your team members you chose in your earlier chapter, I recommend consulting a good tax professional and legal assistant to get individualized advice. Do your research to find a tax advisor who can work with you on this important financial move. Not every CPA understands how you can run your day-to-day life like a business.

Limited Liability Corporation

A Limited Liability Corporation, or an LLC, is a combination of the best parts of a partnership and a corporation. An LLC offers the owners protection from personal liability from any debts the LLC may incur, similar to the structure of a corporation. But an LLC has different tax requirements than a corporation. An LLC is considered a "pass-through" tax entity that does not pay its own taxes. Any profits or losses of the LLC pass through to the LLC owners. The owners in turn report these profits and losses on their tax returns.

Along with the passing through of any profits or losses, the owners of an LLC are protected from personal liability for any debts the business incurs or any claims filed against the business. In other words, if an LLC is unable to pay a creditor, that creditor cannot come after any of the owner of the LLC's personal possessions. This is where the term "limited liability" comes from.

Even though your personal possessions are protected under an LLC, there are still some instances when you can become liable for a debt or a lawsuit. If you directly injure someone, personally guarantee a bank loan, fail to deposit taxes withheld from an employee's wages or intentionally perform fraudulent acts that cause hard to the company, you become liable for your actions.

In addition, if you use the LLC as an extension of your personal affairs, you will also be liable for any debts incurred by the LLC. This is why, if you choose to form an LLC, you must treat it as a business and keep it separate from your personal affairs.

The key tax advantage of creating an LLC is that you don't have to pay taxes on the money that your business spends. Legitimate expenses to your business can become deductions from your business income. This will lower the profits of your business and decrease the amount of taxes you will need to pay.

Corporations

A corporation is a legal entity that is completely separate from its owners. Like an LLC, a corporation offers liability protection. If you form a corporation your personal assets are separate from that of the corporation and you are not personally held responsible for the debts of the company.

Unlike an LLC, a corporation can raise capital by selling shares of stocks. There are some responsibilities that are involved with corporations. In order to remain a corporation, you must hold an annual meeting, take corporate notes and appoint officers.

Like an LLC, a corporation allows you to write-off the expenses of your business. In addition, a corporation is an independent tax entity, separate from the owners and anyone who controls or manages the corporation. Therefore, the owners won't use their personal tax returns to pay tax on any of the corporation's profits. The corporation will pay the taxes on these profits itself. The owners will pay income taxes only on salaries or bonuses received from the corporation.

Benefits of Entities

Regardless of which entity you decide is best for your circumstances, there are advantages in forming either an LLC or a corporation.

- Personal Asset Protection: Both entities allow your personal affairs to be separated from company affairs. This leaves you free and clear from any debts or claims incurred by the company.
- Professional Appearance: The appearance of an "Inc." or an "LLC" after your business name can add authority and convey an image of seriousness and dependability. Potential customers will feel more comfortable doing business with you.

- Name Protection: In the majority of states, no other business can form a corporation or an LLC using the same name of your corporation or LLC.
- Deductions: Normal business expenses can be used as deductions from the profits of the company, allowing for a decrease in taxes.

Systems and Schedules

An inherent difference is that a business has a system and they follow it like clockwork. Getting systemized will create success in itself. All profitable businesses have proven systems. They know who is doing what, when, and how. There are rules, plans, checklists, what-if scenarios, handbooks, guidelines, backup plans, backups for the backup plans, etc.

On a specific day every month set aside a certain amount of time to pay all of your bills, review your budget, assess changes, and make good financial decisions. Don't pay vendors late. Paying vendors late results in penalties or fees and, in the worst case scenario, a complete cut-off of your services. Businesses know this and do everything they can to pay their invoices within thirty days. Likewise, pay your utilities, mortgage, and various other services on time to avoid extra charges.

As you begin to make more money you may have a bookkeeper or accountant pay your bills. This does not mean you don't need to lead them. Now the time you once used paying bills may need to be used overseeing what was paid and how your balance sheet is looking, meeting with your bookkeeper or reviewing your bills and balances. Have a certain month every year to review all insurance policies, wills, loans, and miscellaneous payments. Annually review vendors you have chosen. If those vendors underperform by providing poor service or their prices rise unreasonably, the contract is not renewed. A new vendor is selected. If you are always on top of your finances and have an over view of them monthly and annually you will never be caught off guard. Don't be a failed business. Track your income, build a budget, provide the various "departments" of your life a specific amount of money that they must survive on and stick to it.

There are many applications now that can help us get our lives organized and scheduled. Create a habit to do more by scheduling your day in advance. You must have a systematized way of organizing every major activity in your life. I mean everything from how long you eat breakfast, followed by your morning commute, work, lunch, more work, driving home, dinner, evening activities, exercise, TV shows, sleep, and all the little details in between. Good businesses know where their time is spent. They know where all of their finances are being made and spent. Create a schedule now, and stick to it until it becomes a habit. (Exercise 12)

Organization
Running your life like a business means that you must develop a financial strategy by organizing your finances in the same way a business is organized.

Allocating your funds appropriately and tracking your profits and losses are both important systems that must be in place before you can begin to achieve financial prosperity. Tracking your expenses and income are one step toward running your life like a business. The next step is to continuously monitor your assets and liabilities. Once those steps have become routine, you can make adjustments and minimize your tax liability to increase the flow of cash and allow yourself the freedom to make investments for long-term financial abundance.

PRINCIPLE FOUR -CREATE CASH FLOW

Now that your finances are in order and you have gained control over your spending, you will have a better concept of how much money you have available each month to invest.

Your next project is to create ways to make your money work for you, instead of you always working for your money.

When you first begin saving money it is optimal to put your money aside in a savings account or a money market where it will earn interest and be separated from the money you need for bill-paying and day-to-day spending. But the moment you are ready to move beyond simply saving for an emergency fund, it is time to expand your investments into other vehicles. The interest earned on a savings account or money market fund is minimal and will never provide you with the investment income you need.

In order to accelerate the pace of your financial growth you will need to take non-traditional steps. Your investment portfolio should include stocks, bonds and mutual funds, but you may also want to look at a wider range of options, including real estate. The deeper you look into other opportunities, the greater the possibilities are for choosing investments that will provide you with continuous cash flow.

In earlier chapters we talked about the importance of taking your time to make wise decisions and to develop a team of advisors. As you move forward with further financial decisions, consult with knowledgeable experts who can discuss the pros and cons of each investment opportunity you are considering. Their expertise can reduce your risk when you are deciding which opportunities to fit your investment needs.

When deciding the type of investments to choose for your portfolio, first create standard rules that you will follow. Your rules should be based on how you would like your portfolio to perform for you.

The set of rules provides a guideline you can follow as various investment opportunities present themselves. (Exercise 13)

When it comes knowledgeable investing, the potential for creating a continuous cash flow is limitless. Whether you are a novice investor or already have a performing portfolio, you can always find more opportunities for increasing your cash flow.

One recommendation is to include real estate in your mix of investments. While it is a misperception that the only way to gain great wealth is by owning property, remember that real estate investments provide both a high rate of cash flow and tax benefits. While real estate investing is one venture to consider, there are plenty of other options that can also add to the return on your investment and produce incoming revenue.

You may feel that you don't have enough money to begin investing yet, but don't be fooled. Investing requires only a small amount of cash along with research, commitment, and consistency. Many wealthy investors started out investing tiny sums of money, but as they kept consistently investing year after year they were able to realize consistently greater flows of cash.

Successful investing is a process.

Start by working with what you have, learning which methods work for you, sticking with them and then being flexible enough to accept or decline additional opportunities that can hurt or enhance the performance of your portfolio.

As you grow in confidence you will realize that your pattern should be to invest in opportunities that will, in turn, create more opportunities.

Making Your Money Work for You

Always remember that money attracts more money and more money attracts more opportunities. However, you must make the right choices to maximize those opportunities. If every time you make a profit from one of your investments and you use it in a way that will not bring you additional profit, then you have simply wasted the effort required to obtain that money in the first place.

For example, let's say you work hard for an entire month, saving every penny so that, after careful research, you can make an investment in a lucrative opportunity. At the end of the month, you invest everything in this opportunity. After two months, you find that your initial investment has already doubled in size. At this point, you opt to withdraw your earnings and celebrate with the money until every penny is gone. What you have done is taken your earnings and spent them on things that cannot bring in any more money. In the process, you not only threw out the profits from your investment, but you also tossed away all the money you had saved for that investment on a night of fun. You are now back at square one and will need to scrimp and save again in order to make another investment.

I'm not saying you must hold tight to every penny you receive from investments, but I am saying you must think wisely about what you will do with your profits.

A better way of utilizing those earnings would have been to keep the amount of money you originally invested in the opportunity in order to continue making profits. Take the profits from your initial investment and research another investment opportunity. That way you are creating new ways for more money to come into your life.

Remember, like attracts like .... And money attracts money. Therefore, if you spend all of your earnings you leave nothing for money to be attracted to. If you use it wisely in money-creating ventures, it will come back to you over and over again. It will also eventually afford you the opportunity to have more than just one night of celebration. If you continue to commit yourself to work with your money in this manner you can reach a position in which you can have all that your heart desires.

Follow the Leader

A great way to get started in any arena you are not familiar with or comfortable in is to seek out the path of those who are successful in that area. Read about what they did or how they paved a way for themselves. Were they trailblazers? Did they follow a certain pattern? Did they stay inside the box? Take the time to learn about people whose accomplishments you admire and who you would like to emulate.

After ample research, choose someone who shares your values, responds in a way you would, or did things the way you do them now. Once you have narrowed your search down you can use this person as a role-model until you find someone willing to mentor you or support your training.

Find out what types of investments they chose. How did they get started? What are they doing now? All of this can help you in your efforts to become a successful investor.

Maintain Your Optimism

You may be feeling overloaded with information at this stage and overwhelmed by the demands on your time for research and for developing your financial plans. Stop for a moment, though, to review how far you have already come. You have learned to control your spending and to run your life like a business. You should already be feeling on more solid ground financially. As long as you continue on your current path you will begin to see greater and greater rewards.

It is going to take some time, it is going to take some research and it is going to take some effort and discipline on your end. Think about how beneficial it is going to be on the other side of financial stress, enjoying everything your hard work has gotten you. In fact, once you arrive at your destination of financial freedom, what you feel now to be hard work will seem easy compared to the benefits.

Becoming financially stable isn't an easy feat or a quick task! The people who you see enjoying riches are reaping the rewards of their hard labor and dedication to achieving their goal. It happened for them and it will happen for you. Just put your mind to it, focus on the prize and charge after it will all of your strength and enthusiasm. Not only will you be financially secure, but you can take pride in your determination and accomplishments.

Starting the Investment Cycle

After you have found your "virtual mentor", start to prepare for the investment opportunities you will find through research and word of mouth.

It is a common thought that before you start investing you must pay off all your debt. Not only is this not the correct way of creating wealth, but sometimes this plan can even act as an excuse for you to avoid getting out of your financial rut. You must stick with the plan you previously developed for getting out of debt; however, you *don't* have to wait until you are debt free before you start investing. Investing, while still keeping your debt reduction plan in place, will be valuable because you will be able to use the extra income you have earned from your investments to pay off your debt faster. Adding investment income to the pool of funds you can use to pay off your debt will make it easier and faster than trying to get out of debt with your salary, and remember there is such thing as good debt.

Separate Your Funds

Begin by choosing a monthly amount you can commit to have taken from your earnings, aside from the amount you are using to pay off your debt. This is what financial experts call "paying yourself first." Allocate a certain amount to be separated from your paycheck for investing. "Paying yourself first" might sound as if you could reward yourself with a night out on the town or a trip to the shopping mall.

That is not quite right.

Paying yourself first means giving you an income to be used to create more wealth, not an allowance to be used for leisure activities.

Once you have that amount established, open a savings account at your bank and discipline yourself so that you put that amount in the bank at the end or beginning of each month. One of the easiest methods for ensuring that your savings account builds is to have an automatic system set up with your bank. If your paychecks are direct deposited into your checking account, you can have the deposit split between two accounts or you can simply have the bank transfer a specific amount from checking to savings once or twice each month. It may be easier to have the transfer done twice, each for a smaller amount, as you gradually adjust to the reduction in the amount of money you have available for spending. Once you have reduced your debt, you can increase the amount of money you transfer into savings rather than increasing your spending.

As your savings account balance builds you can continue researching investment opportunities that will create additional income.

Reinvest

As you begin to make investments and see your money grow, reinvest any income you gain from your first investment into other opportunities that will create even more income. This will start your cycle of successful investing and also give you the chance to invest in bigger and better opportunities that will offer higher profits.

Staying disciplined in this cycle will keep your money working for you and give you the opportunity to focus on finding more income to increase your investments.

Guidance

While you ought to rely on your own research and sense of discipline, you also need to consult with the knowledgeable team of experts you developed as you began creating a personal financial plan. Even though you have your "virtual mentor" and have read up on his strategies, you should also have someone who is knowledgeable and can answer your questions and even refer investment opportunities to you. Lawyers, accountants, financial advisors and financial consultants with investment expertise can all prove to be valuable. Look for accountability groups and master mind groups you can consult. They can help you create your investment plan, implement and sustain it.

You've heard it said a wise person surrounds themselves with people who are smarter than they are as a way of learning new ways of doing things.

You have been disciplined in building a substantial amount of money in your investment account but may still be feeling a little nervous about where to invest it. Now you have to trust your research and those you have sought out for guidance.

Diversification

Your research and your advisors and mentors have probably provided you with information about a wide range of investment opportunities. Don't feel you have to choose just one type of investment. You have a lot more to gain if you have many different types of investments in your portfolio. One key to a high-performing portfolio is the willingness of the investor to be flexible and diversified. The classic phrase "don't put all your eggs in one basket" has true value when it comes to investing.

Research Every Opportunity

Your decision to reach for prosperity means you must be responsible for every action you take. You can no longer walk away from an opportunity simply because you don't know enough about it. It is time to research any and every opportunity that is presented to you so that you thoroughly understand its benefits and its shortcomings.

You can no longer allow yourself to just call an investment risky and walk away from it. It is your responsibility to research the opportunity and completely understand why others are calling it risky. Your research may prove to you that the only risk in the investment was you not knowing how it works and how it can perform in your portfolio. Always remember that the more you know about an investment, the more you are able to determine if it will work for you.

Don't forget about the team of knowledgeable people you have developed. You will find that some know more about an area where you are weak and you may know more than they do about another area, such as real estate or a particular business venture. Never overlook those who are within your reach because almost all of the time there will be someone who will be able to provide you with some valuable insight.

Keep in mind the background and motivation of the people you consult. If, for example, you are discussing a particular stock with someone, be sure to question if they will benefit if you choose to invest with them. Don't let yourself be sold. Make sure you consult at least one neutral observer before investing in anything.

Analysis

Have an individualized goal for your investments. While no investment returns can be guaranteed pay attention to the anticipated benefits from a particular investment and then decide if they line up with your objectives.

You may want to build up your net worth or you may want to have a certain amount of cash flow every month. Whatever your objective, be sure the investment you are researching is able to perform accordingly.

When you stick to your requirements you will be more likely to find the opportunities that will lead to your ultimate goals. It's about choosing the right opportunities for your particular situation rather than jumping at every investment that sounds good.

Create an Investment Plan

Throughout this book you have been encouraged to put everything in writing: your values, your financial goals, our expenses, your debts, your income and your assets. Now that you are ready to begin investing, map out a written investment plan. (Exercise 14)

Start by referring back to your written money management plan where you had a list of specific goals and a timeframe to reach those goals. Are there objectives you have not reached such as paying off your bad debt? Place those goals and a time period for accomplishing them at the top of your investment plan. Next, write down your reasons for investing. Next to your reasons, write down the timeframe in which you would like to achieve your results.

Evaluate your Risk Tolerance

Your tolerance for risk is a key factor in determining your investment strategy. Risk tolerance is highly individualized and depends on your income level, your financial responsibilities, your age, your experience and your personality. For example, if you are a novice investor with few obligations and plenty of time to recoup any potential losses, you might be more willing to take on riskier opportunities than someone with a family to feed and low cash reserves. Your goal for retirement enters into this equation, too. If retirement is decades away you can afford to be more adventurous with your money than someone who is five years from retirement and needs to be more protective of their income.

Before you decide you can only tolerate low-risk investments, think about your determination to build your wealth. Opting to be timid and keep all your money in a low-earning savings account will stop you from achieving the prosperity you desire and deserve.

There are a several risk profile tests available in the Internet that you can take to gain some insight into your own tolerance for risk. A few I recommend are:

- http://www.moneymanager.com.au/tools/calculators/investor_quiz.html
- .http://www.walletpop.com/banking/article/_a/bbdp/your-investment-profile/92074
- http://money.cnn.com/magazines/moneymag/moneymag_archive/2002/06/01/323344/index.htm

After you take two or three quizzes you can get a thorough perspective about your tolerance for risk and how that relates to your investment strategy. Write down a summary of your test results and how that will influence the types of investments you ought to choose. Refer to this summary as you continue to make investments.

Now that you understand your investment personality take a moment to recommit yourself to your plan. Underneath your summary of your risk tolerance and your idea of the types of investments that suit your personality, write in bold letters: "I WILL COMMIT TO..." and rewrite the goals you will achieve with your portfolio (Exercise 15).

Now you have reached the stage in which you are ready to move your funds from the safety of your savings account into vehicles that help your money grow faster and increase our cash flow.

Types of Investments

There are a variety of ways you can invest your money. When choosing which ways are right for you and which ones can help you reach your goals, it is important that you know how they perform and research the best strategies for you.

Bonds

Bonds refer to securities that are founded on debt and are considered fixed-income securities. If you were to purchase a bond, you would be lending your money to a company or government. The entity you are lending your money to agrees to pay you interest on your money as well as pay you back the amount you loaned them.

Bonds are a relatively safe investment. However, a downside to bonds is that where there is little risk there is little return. Bonds are not the way to "hit it big." If your tolerance for risk is low, then bonds should definitely be part of your portfolio.

Stocks

When you purchase stocks in a company you become a part owner of the business. This means you get to vote at the shareholders meeting and it also allows you to receive your share of the profits, or dividends, that the company sets aside for its owners.

While bonds can provide a steady stream of income and the peace of mind of know that your investment is somewhat secure, with stocks your initial investment and profit will shift with the market. Stocks go up and down in value daily.

Anyone who follows financial news will recognize the volatility of stocks and the variety of factors that influence their movement. Sometimes a shift in political policies can cause investments to rise and fall, while other times a stock value will change solely because of consumer confidence polling or corporate policies. You can make money from stocks when the value rises, but of course stocks can also lose their value.

Stocks are definitely more risky than bonds, but they also offer the opportunity of reaching your investment goals faster. A moderately aggressive investor could choose to invest in stocks. Some stocks are naturally riskier than others. Use your research and your knowledge of particular industries to choose wisely and your risk could be significantly reduced.

Consult with a financial advisor well-versed in stocks for an additional level of risk reduction.

Mutual Funds

Mutual funds offer a mixture of stocks and bonds. When you invest in a mutual fund, you are pooling your money with a group of other investors. This gives you the opportunity to work with a professional manager who will select investments that are right for the group.

Mutual funds are carefully set up with a particular strategy or focus. Mutual funds invest in anything from large company stocks to start-up businesses to government bonds and international ventures. They vary in terms of aggressive or conservative investments, so you can choose a mutual fund that matches your risk tolerance.

The main advantage of purchasing a mutual fund is that you don't need much investment experience or to spend time evaluating individual opportunities. The professional manager will take care of that. The manager handles the research and investments. However, you still have some responsibilities when you opt to invest in a mutual fund. Your job is to research the mutual fund before you decide to purchase any shares in the fund. Knowing that you chose the right mutual fund for you will allow you to leave the progression of your money in the hands of the fund manager.

You may see a greater return on your investment by purchasing mutual funds due to the fact that you are turning your money over to a professional. This is particularly true for novice investors, since mutual fund managers have more experience in choosing investments.

Mutual fund managers, though, are not always infallible. Mutual fund investments still involve risk and the danger of losing our principal investment. Do you due diligence and make sure you are choosing the best mutual fund you can find that meets your tolerance for risk and yet also has the possibility for increasing your profits. *Money Magazine* and other personal finance publications print an annual list of the best-performing mutual funds.

Be aware that mutual funds charge fees that can decrease your profits. These fees can include the manager's salary, yearly fees and even transaction fees when you purchase or sell shares. While they may seem small on paper, these can definitely add up and reduce your profits. Purchase a mutual fund with careful consideration and a close evaluation of everything entailed, including the fees. A well-researched mutual fund can be a great addition to the portfolio of anyone from a low-risk investor to an aggressive investor.

Annuities

Annuities are an agreement between a consumer and an insurance company that work like a combination of insurance and an investment. The consumer will pay into the annuity either by buying one with a lump sum of money or by paying into the annuity over time; when the annuity purchaser reaches retirement age, the insurance company pays the consumer a specified amount of money over time. All annuities offer tax-deferred growth, with the money you invested available at your retirement. Different types of annuities have different purposes.

Generally, there are three types of annuities:

- Fixed annuities have a guaranteed principal and interest rate. The balance grows on a tax-deferred basis and the benefit is paid at retirement. These are most popular with conservative investors, but the funds are not available until retirement.

- Variable annuities are invested in mutual funds, which may vary in performance, but they also offer some guaranteed life insurance and death benefits.
- Indexed annuities are a hybrid of fixed and variable annuities since some of the funds you contribute are invested in stocks, while there are also some fixed investments.

Annuities should be considered as part of your retirement planning. Consult with an expert in this sometimes complex investment before deciding if this type of investment is something you need in your portfolio. Just remember that annuities will not contribute to your cash flow until you reach retirement age.

Alternative Investments

In addition to stocks and bonds, there are many other alternatives that can create profit. Understanding these will prove to be a little more complicated than the previously discussed investing strategies. These are generally higher in risk but can therefore yield a high profit.

More complex investments are usually not recommended if you are just starting out in investing because they require specialized knowledge. Unless you have done enough research and have a complete understanding of these investments definitely consult an expert who is proficient or you could find yourself losing a lot of money. You definitely don't want or need to jump into the deep end of investing. You can build a strong financial foundation with the basics and then move forward to these more aggressive opportunities if you choose.

Options

Options represent an opportunity to buy or sell something. One person sells options to another, which gives the buyer the right to buy or sell that particular security at a price and time agreed upon by both parties.

The two types of options are "puts" and "calls". A "call" gives the buyer of an option that right to buy an asset, usually a stock, at a specific price within a specific period of time. The buyer purchases the option, hoping that the stock will increase in price before the option expires. If this happens, the buyer can then buy and quickly resell a certain amount of stock (usually specified in the contract) or they can be paid the difference in the stock price when they decide to exercise the option.

A "put" works in the opposite direction, with the buyer of the option being given the right to sell an asset, usually a stock, at a specific price within a specific period of time. Individuals who purchase puts are hoping that the price of the stock will drop before their option expires. This will give them the opportunity to sell it at a price higher than the current market and make a profit.

Options are certainly more intricate than mutual funds or even buying stocks and bonds, and should be reserved for the most advanced investors.

Futures

Futures are contracts on commodities, currencies and stock market indices. They rely on predictions about the value of these securities at some date in the future. Futures are a very high risk investment due to the heavy dependency on speculation. Futures can be used to lock-in a specific price for a future purchase. If the locked-in price is cheaper than the current price, a profit is gained.

FOREX

FOREX refers to the Foreign Exchange Market, a cash market where currencies of nations are traded. The trading often occurs through a hired broker. Foreign currencies are continuously bought and sold across local and global markets and investments can increase or decrease in value based upon currency movements. The market conditions can change at any time as a result of current events. The goal of investors in FOREX trading is to profit from a rise in value of the currency they have purchased.

Real Estate

There is a misconception that anyone who invests in real estate can be on their way to becoming the next Donald Trump. Steer clear of this misperception if you want to prosper in the world of real estate investing. It is not an overnight venture, and it is definitely not a venture that assures great wealth for everyone who chooses to invest in it. As with anything else, real estate investing takes a lot of planning and studying. Although it can be highly profitable, there are many potential pitfalls. However, the more you learn, the less likely you are to fail.

If planned properly, real estate investing can provide a continuous cash flow almost immediately. However, you cannot achieve positive cash flow by going out and buying every cheap house you find. Real estate investing requires strategic planning. You must either learn your local real estate market well or find reliable, trustworthy experts in real estate who can show you where the values are.

Consider working with a group of real estate investment professionals before you attempt to invest in real estate on your own, but don't sit on the side lines too long, you will develop analysis paralysis.

These are just a few examples of the wide range of investments and strategies you can investigate. The more you understand about economic cycles and the likelihood of the profitability of different types of investments in different markets, the more you will be able to take advantage of those cycles as I have.

Some investments will be just right for you. Some will not be good for your situation once you start really researching and looking for purchases to add to your portfolio. An investment plan's different objectives may require different investment strategies. No investment plan is "one size fits all." For specific investment advice, consult a financial advisor or a financial consultant.

Finding a Lucrative Investment

A good way to measure how well an investment will do is to look at its past performance. Let's take mutual funds for example. If you come across a fund that has been making 10% a year for the last 20 years, you could conclude that this fund will continue to perform this way. Never quickly invest in something that you "think" has the potential to make money. If it hasn't proven itself, then wait until it does.

As you begin to invest, you are likely to come across scams that will sound like a good idea. This is why it is so important not to act on impulse. You can go ahead and listen to the details of the opportunity, but be sure to research the track record of the investment and the person offering it to you, and consult with your experts before making any decision. The Internet can also be a great resource for researching a potential investment to be sure it isn't a scam. Never be pushed to make a snap decision, no matter how exciting an investment opportunity sounds.

Many investors find good investments through research, reading and word of mouth, but mostly they rely on a broker or financial advisor or consultant. These consultants are knowledgeable and understand the types of investments that can assist you in creating a portfolio that will perform to your expectations. Financial advisors are also good at informing you about useful tax benefits of particular investment choices.

Be careful, remember they are making money from you, so be sure you know these brokers and advisors and their motivations well.

While consulting with knowledgeable advisors can be valuable, listen with a filter.

Ask yourself:

- Why is this person trying to get me to invest in this particular company, mutual fund, annuity or real estate development?

- Is the person going to make a higher commission because I buy into that product as opposed to another one?
- Does this person own any shares in that investment?

I tell each of my clients to ask the "forbidden questions." You may feel that you are insulting your financial advisor if you question the motivation for any particular advice, but honest, trustworthy advisors want to be open with their clients. An advisor who is uncomfortable with this discussion may not be completely honorable.

In order to avoid being taken by a scam artist or misled by a disreputable advisor, you must have a basic understanding of the different types of investments and how they compare to other investments. This will take work. It may be easier to put your trust in someone else, but that is the best way to lose all of your money. Only invest in something you understand and believe will make money.

Diversifying your Portfolio

Every successful investor has learned that it is best to choose multiple investment opportunities. Some options could be your own business, another business, stocks, gas and oil and definitely real estate. There isn't one set investment that works every time for every investor. There definitely are no "cookie cutter" plans to follow. If there were, you would see far more investors making money far more easily.

Each of our client's portfolios is tailor-made to suit their needs. Each person's vision of the performance of their portfolio is different. Therefore, it is your duty to seek out investment opportunities and decide which ones are right for you. Growing wealth is a process. The more you learn the more your wealth grows. Make it a point to envision the desired profit you wish to receive from your portfolio then learn everything about all of the opportunities that will get you there.

Don't forget the people you sought out along the way who may have necessary information to further your education. Use all of your resources. Wealth is a team sport. Every successful investor had needed the help of others and the many books, magazines, newspapers and television programs with investment information.

Research will not only get you headed in the right direction but it will also take some of the risk out of the opportunities. A few investment tips to remember:

Learn the Market: I cannot emphasize enough the importance of research and of educating yourself. When you become knowledgeable it makes it easier to determine where certain opportunities are headed and if they are a good fit for your portfolio.

Build your Team: Always remember to continue to consult your team of accountants, attorneys, financial advisors and investment counselors. Even as your knowledge of investments grows, you will need the reassurance of your team of consultants. Keep evaluating your consultants to be sure you are working with the team you want. Remember that you are the coach of your team; the leader of your own wealth creation plan.

Pick and Choose: Once you have decided the outcome you would like to see and you know which investments will get you there, focus only on these types of investments. The more narrow your search, the easier it is to gather in-depth information on a specific investment. You can always add other investments in the future.

Watch the Numbers: Take time out to calculate the profits of each investment opportunity and the length of time it will take to obtain them. How do you want your money tied up? Can you get it out? Is there a penalty for making changes to the investment? Get the facts – and remember nothing is guaranteed. It is always better to see the numbers written out rather than estimating them.

Stick to the Plan: Always follow the plan you have created. This is your map to your desired destination. If an opportunity arises that is hyped up by a friend or colleague, always take a moment to make sure it fits into your plan. Don't simply jump in based on someone else's enthusiasm. What is good for someone else may not be good for you.

There will be times when you will encounter uneasiness or feel uncertain about your entire plan. In this case it is best to not make any quick decisions. Evaluate why you are having doubts. Your doubts may pass and you may be extremely happy you waited. It is also possible that your doubts have a legitimate basis. Go back to your making wise decisions steps and consult your team before making changes to your investment plan. Remember that very few investments provide instant gratification.

Active versus Passive Investing

Each investor must decide if they want to be an active investor or a passive investor.

An active investor typically contributes time and devotion to the daily operations of their investment. For example, managing the apartment building you bought, giving input to the business you purchased or even becoming part of the management team.

A passive investor is similar to a silent partner. Passive investors provide the money while other people are responsible for running the operation. With passive investing, you still must stay on top of the profits of your investment. Although you are not part of the daily operations of the venture, you should still be completely aware if the progress and growth of your investment.

Investment Strategies

When you established your investment plan you evaluated your tolerance for risk as well as set your financial goals. Now that we have touched on various potential investments it is time to discuss the three main investment strategies that you can employ to meet your objectives: value, growth and income investing.

Value Investing

Value investing refers to the process of finding opportunities in undervalued businesses or properties. Value investors must do significant research to identify properties that are currently being sold or leased for less than their value. In addition, value investors can buy stock in businesses they perceive are undervalued.

A good example of value investing would be real estate investors with a good track record of flipping houses. A successful value investor will recognize the value in a property that perhaps needs minor repairs or cosmetic improvements. The investors would buy the home for a low price at an auction or at a foreclosure sale or make an offer to a distressed seller, then invest a small amount of time and money to improve the property and sell it within 30 days. For instance, buying a property at $90,000, spending $10,000 for improvements and then selling for $150,000 represents an amazing 50% return on investment.

Income Investing

Individuals interested in earning high dividends are income investors. When investing in stocks, investors operating within this strategy typically prefer a well-established company that will pay earnings to shareholders.

Real estate investors looking to create a continuous flow of income can employ a strategy of buying properties that are valuable for rental income. Again, investors need to find undervalued property, whether residential or commercial, that can be purchased at a below-market price. Whether the properties require improvements or not, the key to successful real estate income investing is to buy property that will be attractive to long-term, high-quality tenants, whether they are businesses or individuals.

Another real estate income investment strategy is based on flipping property. As in the example of value investing, this strategy relies on consistently creating income by buying low, spending minimally on improvements and selling high. A stream of income can be created by continually maintaining a flow of property purchases and sales, even if the profit margin isn't always astronomically high.

Growth Investing

Growth investing is a strategy that focuses on future potential rather than current income. Stock market investors opting for a growth strategy will typically choose new companies or ones that are expanding into new areas.

Real estate investors looking for future growth may want to invest in new communities that are expected to expand. Purchasing land in an area where future retail needs are anticipated or an older commercial site that is ripe for revitalization can work well as part of a long-term growth strategy.

Planning for Retirement

No matter your age or your current financial status, your investment portfolio should include retirement planning. Your long-term goals of creating a continuous flow of wealth and building generational financial stability should include considerations about your future needs.

Work with your team of financial advisors, particularly a tax professional, to evaluate and choose the best place for your retirement savings. Be sure that as you create a money management system for paying off your debt and investing, you are setting aside money in a tax-protected or tax-deferred account that will fund your retirement. Not only can this improve your current tax bill, but the money can be used in your retirement years as part of your cash flow strategy. If you are employed by a company that provides additional matching funds for a 401K, be sure to take full advantage of this free money.

Multiple types of IRA accounts are available to individuals whether they are self-employed or not. A tax consultant and your research can help you choose the type of IRA that best meets your individual circumstances.

Individualized Investing

As you have seen, each investor's strategy should be highly individualized according to their needs and their goals. Your personality and tolerance for risk enters into the decision-making process along with the advice you receive from financial advisors and consultants.

As you move forward with your financial plan you may find that your risk tolerance and your investment strategy adjust. If you initially invest in order to increase your cash flow, as your income increases and you reduce your debt you may be more interested in building your net worth. As your confidence grows in your ability to make wise investment decisions you may find yourself less averse to more aggressive investment strategies.

The same way you took a moment to envision your life the way you want it, now take a moment to visualize the desired results you wish to achieve with your investments. Ask yourself why you are investing in the first place. Make sure every opportunity you choose to invest in aligns with your answer to that question. Always do your research and move cautiously with the advice of your group of experts and your standards to guide you. The more you invest, the easier it will become to recognize which ventures are right for you.

PRINCIPLE FIVE -MONEY DOES GROW ON TREES

There are exactly two types of people: those who are able to read this chapter's title aloud with complete conviction and those who cannot.

Even if you have fully embraced the principles of this book and recognize the power of positive thinking, you may still be having trouble with the phrase "Money does grow on trees."

Having started on your path to prosperity, you are fully aware of the importance of making wise decisions and basing those choices on in-depth research and the advice of your trustworthy team. All this requires work, not just snatching cash as it drops into your lap.

Think back to the beginning of your journey.

Before you were able to begin developing your prosperity plan, you had to change your mindset. The foundation for your future relies on eliminating negative feelings and developing a positive attitude.

Remember hearing your parents say, "Money doesn't grow on trees"? To our parents, this statement was part of the process in teaching us to be frugal and careful with our money.

But this statement is a prime example of negative thinking.

How can we ever become abundant and prosperous when we are bombarded with negative thinking? Flipping this statement and embracing an affirmative, positive attitude is the most empowering action any of us can take.

In this chapter we will expand on the concept of opening our minds to an ever-expanding range of opportunities.

This may be the most challenging, yet most rewarding, step on your path to prosperity. Changing our outlook and mindset requires a decision and dedication to that decision.

When we successfully make and embrace change, we have the ability to control our financial future **and** we will be able to say with conviction, "Money *does* grow on trees."

Expect to Encounter Change

Throughout history, people believed in an idea as the absolute truth, only to discover they were mistaken. At one time, people firmly believed that the world was flat and existed as the center of the solar system. Now we know the "truth" and even that may change in time. Be unafraid to explore something about which you were once skeptical. Without that exploration, there can be no growth.

Just as the collective world continues to correct or adapt inaccuracies in the name of progress, we do the same for our own personal histories.

In your lifetime of experiences, how many prior beliefs or systems of doing things needed to evolve or completely change over time as newly discovered information or situations arose? Adapting can be as simple as changing your route when you discover a road is closed. Adapting can also be extremely frustrating. Consider the teacher who used the same teaching methods for thirty years suddenly being asked to immediately integrate a new instruction technique into her classroom. She would find it difficult.

Whether the changes we need to make are easy or hard, the sooner we realize that change is inevitable and unavoidable in all aspects of life, the more prepared and open to it we become.

By knowing to expect change, identifying even minor variances and adapting to them becomes natural, even easy, making transitions smoother. The further out we anticipate change, the earlier we can plan for it.

Consider the situation of the closed road mentioned earlier. What if the unaware driver, never anticipating a change in his routine, was driving on autopilot (as many people do when they are traveling a familiar route) and missed the detour signs. That driver would only discover the road closure when the asphalt was blocked by orange cones. If, instead, he were fully taking in his surroundings and looking proactively for change, he would have seen the detour signs earlier, avoided backtracking, and been on time for his destination. This example may seem simplistic, but it reveals a slice of human nature.

Ignore the possibility of change and we will be blindsided by it.

Pay attention to the possibility of change and we will be ready for anything life throws at us.

Applying the "expect change" mentality to the business side of our lives means to always look ahead and seek new opportunities. The most successful people read, research, and keep up with the information that is most beneficial to their prosperity.

Yet, research alone is not enough.

Successful entrepreneurs know that being ready for change is an important part of doing their due diligence and will directly affect their chances of success. Rather than accepting your current situation or your current investment strategy as stagnant, become a forward-thinking individual who is aware of the possibilities for career advancement, real estate purchases, and other opportunities for making money.

Regardless of what business you are in, staying "on top of your game" always puts you in a position of power. All paths to prosperity must assume change as elemental. Our awareness of change is a critical part of the process. Continue to challenge what you think you know by stepping out of your comfort zone. For example, if you think you only understand residential real estate and that commercial real estate investing is not for you, take the time to recognize how the two industries are related.

Your expertise in one area could lead you to great success in another. When you take off your blinders, you might be amazed at the new things you observe and how your surroundings expand.

Masking

Struggling with change is a natural human condition. Even after they learn to expect change, many people still handle it with a way of behaving that I call masking. Essentially, it is another way we struggle with change rather than embrace it.

Often, we try to create the perfect picture of what order is to us. If we attain it, we try to maintain it, but eventually we recognize that nothing is permanent. The athlete at the top of his game, with a happy family life at home and his favorite new car in the driveway may think that this phase of his life will go on forever, but he needs to be ready for his next move. The homeowner can cut the grass and pull the weeds and plant vegetables and assume the garden is set for the year, but the grass and the weeds will grow back and the vegetables will need to be harvested. You can pretend that life won't change and you can buy fake grass and grocery store vegetables, but these actions only mask the real issue. Humans as a species have trouble accepting impermanence.

Change happens. It can't be stopped.

For trivial issues such as lawn care, various masking solutions can be effective, but masking will never be effective when it comes to your prosperity. There is no amount of masking that will be beneficial to you. We can't throw bills away and pretend they don't exist. We can't cross out one number on our bank statements and fill in something larger.

Do you remember the children's story about the squirrel that nailed and taped all the leaves to the trees in an effort to prevent winter from coming, instead of gathering nuts and preparing for the cold months? That squirrel was successful in masking the look of winter, but it came as it always does and he was without food. He had to rely on the kindness of other animals that winter. The squirrel's story demonstrates an important lesson for all ages; stop fighting change and embrace it instead. The sooner you accept and learn the best ways to handle life's changes, the sooner you will be prosperous. When we mask realities, we create additional obstacles that keep us from prosperity.

Impermanence

"We are either progressing or retrograding all the while. There is no such thing as remaining stationary in this life." – James Freeman Clarke

Nothing in life is stagnant. We must either adapt and prosper or fall behind. If you feel yourself spinning wheels and losing optimism without getting anywhere, you are not modifying your pace enough to move forward. In addition to being aware of and expecting external changes outside of your control, you must make personal changes, both physically and mentally, to maintain your positive development and personal growth. These changes are also crucial elements in the equation of success. Every successful person already knows this. Although it is a simple notion, the act of change is anything but simple. We are all creatures of habit and we have to eliminate those bad habits before true success can be achieved.

Habits

We all have habits. Some are sensible, others ridiculous, and we are attached to every single one of them.

As we age the more attached we become. Have you ever noticed that the older someone is, the more often her way becomes the right way? If it seems as if the elderly grow increasingly resistant to change, it is often because they are. The reason for this is simple. The longer we repeat habits, the more deeply engrained they become, as well as harder to part with.

Consciously or unconsciously, we become what our habits dictate through our actions, speech, and thoughts. To make way for prosperity to unfold, we learn to modify some habits, eliminate others and begin to build new ones. The older we are the harder this will be. Habits make us who we are, remind us where we came from, and guide us toward where we are destined to travel.

Changing our habits directly changes our lives and is a process that takes time and conscious effort.

Science of Habits

Remember the driver who was not paying enough attention to notice the detour signs? Most absentminded behavior is due in part to natural habit-forming tendencies. Our brains learn and perform most effectively from repetition and practice. The more time and effort spent learning something, the more hardwired and natural it becomes. That's why piano teachers insist that their students practice daily and why math teachers demand memorization of multiplication tables.

Starting at birth repetitions (identified at first by our senses) begin to create neural connections. This is how babies start to recognize their fathers and mothers by their voices and scents. The connections become increasingly stronger with each additional repetition. These connections develop our minds and fill them with thoughts, consciousness, memories, and habits. The more exposure and experience we collect, the easier these tasks become.

Think about the driver on his way to work using the same route he has taken every weekday for more than two years at the same time of day and in the same car he has driven for three years. His body has developed and mastered that habits necessary to effectively travel that route, at that time, in that car, with the least amount of attention required.

Some tasks become so easy for us to accomplish we almost forget we are even doing them. If you ever space out or daydream while driving and find yourself at your destination without even remembering the drive itself, you have experienced this phenomenon. Our habits have simply taken over for us, allowing us to multitask; nature's way of simplifying things. It takes time for this phenomenon to strengthen. Think back to when you first drove a car. You were not able to allow your mind to think about other things as a more experienced driver can sometimes do.

Aside from the few individuals who have a natural, innate musical or athletic ability, most people experience a learning curve for any new activity at any stage in life. As an example, I wasn't born walking but I am able to walk better now than I could as a toddler. As a toddler, each of us has to use every ounce of brain power to focus just on walking without falling down or banging into anything because our brains were processing so many new experiences. By the time we advanced beyond the toddler stage, our brains processed everything associated with the task of walking. Children learn to walk differently on sand or grass than on concrete. By the time we are adults, most of us can walk or even run on a treadmill while watching television, looking at a magazine, talking on a cell phone, or listening to music on an iPod.

Our abilities improve with every repetition. Each time we repeat an action successfully it becomes more automatic and habitual. By the time we are adults we don't think about how to walk or how to sit up or stand up, these are all natural movements that we learned through repetition from a young age.

While automatic responses can free our minds to make them available for other thoughts and activities, habits can present problems when a typical situation changes in some way. Have you ever rented or borrowed a car with a gearshift in a different location than your own car? Once, I drove a friend's car for a week and every single time I sat in the driver's seat I'd grab at the space between the seats even though I knew by then that the gearshift was behind the wheel. My automatic responses were useless and irritating. Even though my eyes saw the gearshift, my muscle memory moved my hand to the accustomed location.

Automatic responses only improve our performance efficiency in familiar situations.

Adapting to New Situations

Now that we understand how determined our minds can be to hold onto our habits, you can be more understanding of yourself as you begin to change your mental outlook. Changing your mindset does not happen overnight.

Fortunately, just like driving and walking, breaking habits and making changes gets easier with practice.

When we attempt to eliminate old ideas or methods and replace them with something entirely different, we use the same process of repetition and practice that we used to develop those ideas and methods in the first place. Unfortunately, it is easier to learn than to unlearn habits, especially when we factor in our age or the strength of that habit. Think about how much simpler it was to *start* biting your nails than it was to *quit* that habit.

Those who expect to grow and succeed learn to adapt. Change helps our minds become stronger and more agile. Our minds need exercise just as much as our bodies. Just as muscle confusion builds a stronger body, challenging our minds works out our brains and keeps them in peak operating condition. Eventually, what was once a challenge becomes easy. What was unthinkable becomes possible. Continuing to build our mental resources strengthens our chance of success.

Breaking Bad Habits

Now that we have a basic understanding of how habits work, let's identify the changes we can make to our own thinking. The most important will be to switch from negative thinking to positive thinking.

Most people feel they have an innate personality trait as an optimist or a pessimist. But even the most pessimistic person can change their thought processes to become more positive. Of course, it is much easier for an optimist to devote his mind to positive patterns. A pessimist may find that forcefully adjusting from a "deficiency" mentality to a mind full of positive, abundant thoughts requires time and energy. Remember, that habit of negative thinking can be unlearned.

Imagine how easy it would be if we could "copy," "paste," or "delete" when processing the contents of our minds just as we do on our computer documents. Unfortunately, we can't download an update from the Internet to manipulate our thoughts but there is a system available to break down old habits.

Power of the Tongue

Monitoring our speech is one of the best places to start breaking bad habits and eliminating negativity. One of our greatest potential strengths in life resides directly under our noses. Our capacity for speech is an extraordinary gift of power. Life and death are in the power of the tongue, depending on how we develop and use that power. Our words are so powerful that they can bless or curse, encourage or discourage, heal or hurt, build up or tear down others and ourselves. Our words influence the way we act and feel and help determine our attitude and outlook on life.

We have to be careful of the words we use in day-to-day conversations. We may not be aware of it, but the everyday words we use turn into our beliefs and our actions. Our words act as a way of telling our subconscious what to believe. They are daily affirmations that affect the outcome of our lives. If we continue to talk in a negative way, we are creating the formation of negativity in our lives. From now on, instead of saying you are *trying* to do something, say you *are* doing it. Rather than say, "I am *trying* to become financially abundant", say, "I **will** be financially abundant." Not, "I *want* to buy a house", but, "I **will** buy a house."

Even saying a positive phrase aloud can evoke a feeling of happiness, excitement, and commitment to have whatever it is you want. Positive affirmations are a way of saying yes to your goals.

Repeat to yourself, "I **will** accomplish my goals."

Mantras and the repetition of phrases are so effective because they divert the mind from distraction and focus it on the sounds and words our mouths are creating. Mantras and positive affirmations eliminate stress, lower blood pressure, and affect who we are because of the direct physical and mental effects of our speech on our minds and bodies. Medical research shows that the part of the brain that controls speech has connections with every nerve of the body.

This explains why the words you say affect your health, your prosperity and your belief in yourself. Every part of your body connects with the speech area. Therefore, we need to be thoroughly aware not only of everything we think, but also of everything we say. Did your parents and teachers ever tell you to "think before you speak"? That's excellent advice to help you avoid hurting someone's feelings by blurting out a criticism or sharing someone else's secret.

When you "think before you speak" you can also take the time to choose to think and speak in a positive, life-affirming way for your own benefit. Try saying some of the following statements out loud to yourself:

- I am healthy.

- I am wealthy.
- I am prosperous.
- I am a good wife.
- I am a good husband.
- I am a good parent.
- I am a good friend.

You should immediately begin to feel better and believe in yourself and your abilities. Experts say "depression hurts" for a reason. Being down in thought and speech takes a serious toll on our bodies and our lives.

While everyone has experienced a slip of the tongue and said something they regret later, we can all train our minds and our mouths to stop making negative statements. Even a few spoken negative words can take us off our desired course.

Let's use piloting an airplane as an example. If the pilot sets the course just a degree or two off target, the plane won't arrive at the proper destination. At the beginning of the flight, a few degrees might not seem to matter, but the longer the pilot neglects to correct that error, the veers further and further off course until the final destination is nowhere in sight. Be very careful with your words and your thoughts.

Words used correctly will turn on the life cycle, the health cycle, and the overall prosperity cycle. Words used incorrectly will turn on the death cycle, deficiency cycle, fear cycle, and sickness cycle.

Conceiving words in your heart and then speaking them aloud will plant a seed. It is up to you to do what is required to help these seeds grow. Be extremely careful to project the things you desire while removing the thoughts you want to separate from your life.

Think about the many ways speaking negatively can have serious implications. If a reputable newspaper ran a fabricated story or published false gossip about someone and then printed a retraction the next day, the paper's reputation is still tarnished. In jury trials, words are used by the attorneys to sway the jurors' perceptions of the guilt or innocence of the defendant. Both sides will manipulate the evidence gathered for the case, sometimes even presenting false or misleading information that they know will eventually be stricken from the record. They do this because the jurors will remember what they have heard. Even if the judge tells them to forget the evidence that was expunged from the trial record, most jurors will be unable to erase their memory.

Words linger.

In high school, a teacher organized a lesson in which all the students formed a circle around a large piece of paper with a picture of a girl drawn on it. The teacher instructed each student to verbally insult the girl in the picture and then crinkle up a piece of the paper. By the time the students were finished, the girl and the paper were one big paper ball. Next, the teacher had each student do the opposite: give the picture of the girl a compliment and smooth out part of the paper. At the end of the exercise, the paper was no longer a giant ball, but the picture of the girl remained wrinkled beyond repair. This exercise demonstrated just how damaging negative speaking can be, even when someone tries to counterbalance it with a positive comment.

Redemption from the negative takes a long time to acquire. Start now by training yourself to speak only positive words. (Exercise 16) Your words are like dynamite. They will have explosive effects on your life and on your prosperity that can be positive or negative. Which would you prefer?

Exude Positivity

"Human beings, by changing the inner attitudes of their minds, can change the outer aspects of their lives."

– William James

In addition to managing our words, we must now begin the process of successfully and permanently changing our mindset from "I cannot" to "I can". Only after achieving the "I can" mantra will we be able to build upon its foundation. (Exercise 17) An optimistic, positive attitude is something we can refer back to and rely on when obstacles present themselves. Think about the children's story, "The Little Engine that Could," where the train engine in that story achieves success by believing in herself and her ability. She repeats *I think I can, I think I can,* over and over until she realizes *I **know** I can* by the end of the story.

Positive thinking is powerful. Does this mean that all your greatest hopes and dreams will fall into your lap just because you're a positive person and spin everything in a positive light?

Of course not.

If simply replacing negative feelings with positive ones brought immediate success, there would be no need for this book. Everyone would be prosperous and successful. Positive thinking is an important part of the impetus to *making yourself* successful. Believing that you have the intelligence and determination to become prosperous provides the backbone to make the wise decisions and changes to your life that are required to build generational wealth and to improve every aspect of your life.

Not everyone in life chooses to win. Some people stay negative and believe that their lack of success is someone else's fault. Sophocles said, "Success is dependent on effort."

Replace your negative thoughts with positive thoughts but don't stop there. The most effective way to build on positivity is to convince yourself that you can do whatever is required in your plan to reach prosperity. Being confident and knowing that you can succeed in every endeavor is the first step. Positivity will come in handy when you hit bumps in the road. Frederick Douglass once said, "If there is no struggle, there is no progress."

Recognize that there will be obstacles to overcome, but depend on your positive outlook and your prosperity plan to maintain your motivation. Remember the exercise in the introduction when we turned negative statements about money into positive affirmations? Refer back to that page of affirmations you wrote in the back of this book at least once each day and contemplate the meaning of each statement. The more time you spend on this activity, the sooner you will reach your goal of prosperity.

Quitting the Blame Game
We all do it.
And it has to stop.

What am I talking about? Making an excuse for why we cannot do things because it is simply that…an *excuse.*

If we really want to achieve something, it is usually possible. If you don't have desire and you are simply not driven or goal-oriented, that is perfectly fine, but stop complaining about things you never really tried to attain. I can never understand why people are so afraid of mental work. They will damage themselves with physical work, but are afraid to prosper more and work less. No one wants to live in the poor house, but if you ask someone to research an investment they will give you ten reasons why they cannot do it.

Excuses don't do anything for us but keep us from moving ahead. Those who blame other people and other circumstances for their own faults and the things they lack are weak. Many people feel as though life happens to them, for good or bad and that things are out of their control. This way, when anything goes wrong, they don't have to take responsibility for their failure. Instead, they blame bad luck.

The "woe is me" attitude simply does not exist in strong people. Strong people have the courage to do their best to control a situation and make the best of it. It's not as if bad things don't happen to these people. They have learned to handle adversity in a different way, turning their obstacles into success stories.

Resilient people experience an incredible feeling when they overcome obstacles. Think back to a time in your life when you had to handle something difficult. Even if this were as small an occasion as dealing with another student who had stolen your idea for a school project or as large as having to admit to a damaging mistake you made at work.

How did you feel about facing up to the challenge? Did your confidence grow because of the experience?

Going through life with no opposition and no obstacles sounds like a great life, but then we would never learn and grow from our mistakes. You would never know the powerful feeling of having succeeded at something because you truly devoted yourself to it. When we give our best, even if we don't succeed, no one can say we did not try. When we try, we go further than when we don't try at all.

Application

"The level of thinking that got you to where you are now will not get you to where you dream of being."
–Albert Einstein

Positive thinking has to be applied consistently every day, every hour, every minute. Your focus while reading this book has been on making wise financial decisions, but the lessons about the power of a positive attitude and positive speaking can be helpful to you in other aspects of your life.

Once you have turned your mind over to optimism and are open to new and positive opportunities for building your wealth you will find that this mindset spills over into every aspect of your life.

We've come a long way since you began reading this book. If you've started the implementing the exercises and advice in this book, your future should already look more certain and you will be on your way to achieving the goals you have set for yourself. Stay on top of your affairs and keep your team of motivators and advisors close at hand.

Life, as you know it, has probably already changed for the better. It is about to change even more. You have everything you need to succeed. Now all you have to do is continue to maintain your motivation and your willpower.

Resolve to know everything about your finances at all times. Seek out new ventures. Create new ways of making money. Always leave room for additional advisors and mentors rather than restricting yourself to the people you originally found. Not only should you be flexible and open to new opportunities, but your team should be as well.

Keep your finances in order so that you are running your life like a business. Realize that you are now in business for yourself. Even if you have another job, you are in the business of making money. Run your business so that it becomes a cycle that will continually generate more money.

This chapter has reinforced the importance of developing good habits and making wise decisions and truly believing in your own courageous strength and ability to prosper. Among those good habits should be a continual cycle of gathering more knowledge and information about the world. Learn about real estate and potential business investments. Study the financial sections of magazines and newspapers. No truly successful investor ever remains stagnant. New opportunities are available every day. The more you know, the more likely you are to find higher paying ventures and to explore new avenues.

Pay it Forward

Pass on your knowledge and experience to others, especially your own children. If you don't have kids, consider sharing your knowledge with colleagues and friends and mentoring other children.

If you do have children, set up savings accounts for them and give them opportunities to make money so they can save it for the future. Educate them on the correct practices of creating financial stability so they won't have to suffer through so many of the pitfalls that most of us have struggled with.

Now that you have decided to change your life for the better, remind yourself often of your goals. Enjoy each milestone you achieve on your personal path to prosperity.

If you hand someone a fish they eat for a day, but if you teach them to fish, they eat for a lifetime.

EXERCISES

The Prosperity Principles

Positive Money Views:
(Write your positive views of money here. Read these aloud every day.)

Exercise 1: Evaluate Your Decisions

Think about the poor decisions you have made. Pick up a pencil and a pen because you will need both. You can use the blank pages at the back of this book for this exercise. Now, in pencil write down a bad decision and the outcome. Underneath it, in pen, write down what the better decision might have been and some possible outcomes. Your chart should like this:

Bad Decision (write in pencil- these are not permanent decisions) As you learn to make better decisions you can erase the bad ones you made in the past.	Outcome
Better Decision (write in pen – these are permanent better choices)	Outcome

When you do this exercise, it is important not to dwell on "What if" but to learn from your mistakes. Decide why you think your decision was a mistake, figure out what made you choose that path and then turn this experience around into a positive outcome.

Now, there may be nothing you can do about lost money from a bad investment, but if you understand where your thinking went wrong you can visualize the possibility of future, successful investments. The important thing is not to focus on the negative outcomes of earlier decisions but to stay positive about your potential. You are going to make great decisions.

As my mother often told me, "So you made a bad decision. Now, make a different, **better,** decision."

Exercise 2: Create a Financial Balance Sheet
Balance Sheet

What are your financial goals this year?

What are you invested in that is making you money?

Income			Assets		
Source		Amount	Source		Amount
TOTAL		$ -	TOTAL		$ -

Expenses			Liabilities		
Source		Amount	Source		Amount
TOTAL		$ -	TOTAL		$ -

Estimated Net Worth		$

How can you improve this chart?

Set New Financial Goals:

Exercise3: Write Down Your Goals

Goals →→Decisions→→ Thoughts→→ Action

Write your goals on one of the blank pages at the back of this book. You may want to copy your list on other pages of paper to keep in a place where you will see them every day.

First, categorize your goals. For example, my categories for goals are: Spiritual, Family, Financial, Physical/Health, Social/Friendships. Your categories may be different. Be generous in coming up with your categories to make sure you cover every part of your life.

Next, start every goal with the phrase "I will." Be specific. Then determine what it will take to reach that goal.

Here's an example to show you what I mean:

Goal: **I will make $500,000 by December 31.** (This assumes you are writing your goals in January.)

- I will make $41,666.67 per month.
- I will make $10,416.67 per week.
- I will make $2,083.33 per day (based on a five-day week)
- I will make $26.42 per hour (based on an eight-hour day)
- I will generate $1.4 million in sales per month (based on a 3% commission)
- I will sell four $350,000 houses per month
- I will make 20 phone calls per day

- I will send out 1000 emails per day
- I will meet four new people per week
- I will keep a daily blog and inform my clientele of new homes for sale

Do this for every goal you have and put them somewhere where you can see them and WILL read them every day.

Write down a few of your goals here:

Exercise 4: Finding Your Top Six Values

Study the values listed on the following pages.

Pick your top 100 values, even if it is a maybe, keep it in. Then narrow your list to 50, 25,10,6.

Make sure your top six values are really your core values and justify why.

Abundance	Beauty	Composure
Acceptance	Being the best	Concentration
Accessibility	Belonging	Confidence
Accomplishment	Benevolence	Conformity
Accuracy	Bliss	Congruency
Achievement	Boldness	Connection
Acknowledgement	Bravery	Consciousness
Activeness	Brilliance	Consistency
Adaptability	Buoyancy	Contentment
Adoration	Calmness	Continuity
Adventure	Camaraderie	Contribution
Affection	Capability	Control
Affluence	Care	Conviction
Aggressiveness	Carefulness	Conviviality
Agility	Celebrity	Coolness
Alertness	Certainty	Cooperation
Altruism	Challenge	Cordiality
Ambition	Charity	Correctness
Amusement	Charm	Courage
Anticipation	Chastity	Courtesy
Appreciation	Cheerfulness	Craftiness
Approachability	Clarity	Creativity
Assertiveness	Cleanliness	Credibility
Assurance	Clear-mindedness	Cunning
Attentiveness	Cleverness	Curiosity
Attractiveness	Closeness	Daring
Availability	Comfort	Decisiveness
Awareness	Commitment	Deference
Awe	Compassion	Delight
Balance	Completion	Dependability

Depth
Desire
Determination
Devotion
Devoutness
Dexterity
Dignity
Diligence
Direction
Directness
Discipline
Discovery
Discretion
Diversity
Dominance
Dreaming
Drive
Duty
Eagerness
Economy
Education
Effectiveness
Efficiency
Elation
Elegance
Empathy
Encouragement
Endurance
Energy
Enjoyment
Entertainment
Enthusiasm
Excellence
Excitement
Exhilaration
Expertise
Exploration
Fairness
Faith
Fame
Family
Fascination
Fashion

Fearlessness
Ferocity
Fidelity
Financial
Independence
Firmness
Fitness
Flexibility
Flow
Fluency
Focus
Fortitude
Frankness
Freedom
Friendliness
Frugality
Fun
Generosity
Gentility
Giving
Grace
Gratitude
Gregariousness
Growth
Guidance
Happiness
Harmony
Health
Heart
Helpfulness
Heroism
Holiness
Honesty
Honor
Hopefulness
Hospitality
Humility
Humor
Hygiene
Imagination
Impact
Independence
Industry

Ingenuity
Insightfulness
Inspiration
Integrity
Intelligence
Intensity
Intimacy
Intuition
Intuitiveness
Investing
Joy
Judiciousness
Justice
Kindness
Knowledge
Leadership
Learning
Liberation
Liberty
Liveliness
Logic
Longevity
Love
Loyalty
Majesty
Making   a
difference
Mastery
Meekness
Meticulousness
Mindfulness
Modesty
Motivation
Mysteriousness
Neatness
Open-mindedness
Openness
Optimism
Order
Organization
Originality
Outlandishness
Outrageousness

Passion
Peace
Perceptiveness
Perfection
Perkiness
Perseverance
Persistence
Persuasiveness
Playfulness
Pleasantness
Pleasure
Poise
Polish
Popularity
Power
Practicality
Pragmatism
Precision
Preparedness
Presence
Privacy
Professionalism
Prosperity
Prudence
Punctuality
Purity
Realism
Recognition

Recreation
Refinement
Reflection
Relaxation
Reliability
Religiousness
Resilience
Resolution
Resolve
Resourcefulness
Respect
Rest
Restraint
Reverence
Richness
Rigor
Sacredness
Sacrifice
Sagacity
Saintliness
Sanguinity
Satisfaction
Security
Self-control
Selflessness
Self-reliance
Sensitivity
Serenity

Service
Sexuality
Sharing
Shrewdness
Significance
Silence
Silliness
Simplicity
Sincerity
Skillfulness
Solidarity
Solitude
Soundness
Speed
Spirituality
Spontaneity
Stability
Stealth
Stillness
Strength
Structure
Success
Support
Supremacy
Surprise
Sympathy
Synergy

Exercise 5: Do Your Goals and Values Line Up?

Remember, your values are who you are and will continue to help you achieve greater things. Your goals will get you there so they need to line up. I've given you an example for myself, now you do your six values and on the goal side say how they correlate, this will help you know your values are in line with your goals and will confirm you are on the right path for change.

Values

Loyalty	*Bible study daily* *Dedication to my family* *Committed to my finances* *Maintain healthy weight and body*

Exercise 6: Understanding the Decision

8 Steps to Decision Making

Step One: What Type of Decision is it?

- Yes/No Decision
- Options Decision
- Only If Decision

Step Two: The Ways Decisions Are Made

- Intuition (No)
- Pattern (No)
- Follow (No)
- Logical (Yes)

Step Three: Why Am I Making This Decision?

Step Four: Is Something Worrying Me About This Decision?

Why Am I Worried or Afraid?
Be Honest
Expect a Challenge
Stay Positive
Stay Focused

Step Five: Ask the four questions

1. Will this purchase or decision help me get to my destination/goal?
2. Have I given this decision enough thought?
3. Have I done my research on every option of my decision?
4. Does it line up with my goals and values?

MAKING THE DECISION

Step Six: Research the Facts

Establish Your Goals
Establish Your Values
Set Your Criteria
Develop Alternatives
Assess the Risk

Step Seven: Be Clear About What to Decide

Step Eight: Know What Kind Of Result You Want

Exercise 7: Who are Your TEAMmates

What TEAMmates do you need? List as many as you need today. Understand this list will change as your needs change. Reevaluate this list every year and add or subtract to it as necessary.

1.
2.
3.
4.
5.
6.
7.
8.
9.
10.

Exercise 8: Interview and Evaluate Your Advisors

What are the main questions you want to ask your advisors in order for you to know they are the most qualified professional to help you? For each person you chose to put on your TEAM, write down at least three questions that will help you understand if they are the correct person for you.

Professional:

Financial Advisor	1. Are you licensed and Registered with FINRA 2. How much money do you currently manage? 3. Are you a risk taker or conservative?

Exercise 9: Schedule Regular Meetings

When are your scheduled meetings to review your wealth plan? The larger your portfolio, the more often they may need to be. Give specific dates; put them in your calendar. Don't forget about reviewing your insurance policies, 401K, goals, etc.

Exercise 10: Create a Budget

Monthly Expense	Budget	Actual
Deductions		
Savings (to set aside)	$	$
Child Support, Alimony etc.	$	$
Other:	$	$
Housing		
Rent or Mortgage payment	$	$
Utilities	$	$
Home Insurance & Taxes	$	$
Other:	$	$
Debt Payment		
Credit Card Payments (min)	$	$
Other Loans:	$	$
Food		
Groceries	$	$
Eating Out	$	$
Coffee & Bar	$	$
Other:	$	$
Transportation		
Car Payment	$	$
Car Insurance + Taxes	$	$
Car Maintenance	$	$
Gas	$	$
Public Transit, Parking, Tolls	$	$
Other:	$	$
Family		
Day Care & Babysitting	$	$

Activities & Lessons	$	$
Allowances & Child Support	$	$
Other:	$	$
Personal & Health		
Clothing	$	$
Toiletries & Care Products	$	$
Haircuts	$	$
Gym & Sport Club Dues	$	$
Health, Life, etc. Insurance	$	$
Doctor & Dentist Visits	$	$
Prescription & OTC Drugs	$	$
Other:	$	$
Education		
Tuition	$	$
Books & Fees	$	$
Supplies	$	$
Other:	$	$
Entertainment		
Tickets for Shows & Games	$	$
Books & Magazine subscr.	$	$
DVDs, CDs, Video Games	$	$
Other:	$	$
Miscellaneous		
Charity, Gifts & Offerings	$	$
Pet Supplies & Vet	$	$
Entertaining Guests	$	$
Cash not Accounted for	$	$
Other:	$	$

Summary Calculation

Monthly **Net** Income	$	$
- Expenses Total	$	$
= **Monthly Spendable Income**	$	$

Exercise 11: Good Debt vs. Bad Debt

Create a chart and on one side list your good debt, on the other list your bad debt and a plan to eliminate it. You may not have that plan right away, so leave it blank until you have a plan you can commit to. If you don't have a plan today, set a goal, a date when you will be able to fill in the "eliminating bad debt action steps" column. List your bad debt in order of what you want to pay off first. Remember, once you have that first debt paid you are going to allocate more money to the next debt until you are completely debt free.

Good Debt	Bad Debt	Plan
House	*10K Credit Card*	*Pay $200 above the minimum payment*

Exercise 12: Create a Daily/Weekly/Monthly Schedule and Stick to It

We must schedule our time to be successful. In today's day and age we can schedule on our phones, on calendars, in Outlook or programs like Outlook. Find a system that works for you and schedule out each day. Don't forget your monthly or annual meetings with your TEAM members. This will help you schedule your time and will actually give you more free time to spend with your loved ones. I even schedule my free days and what I am doing for fun.

Exercise 13: What Are Your Investing Rules?

Think about what is the minimum you want to make. Do you want to be an active or a passive investor? What is necessary for you to deem this investment successful? Think of five investment rules you will adhere to.

1.
2.
3.
4.
5.

Exercise 14: When is Enough Enough?

What is your goal?

Age/dollar amount/ cash flow amount…etc.

Be as specific as possible here. Remember, a goal that is not written down is just a dream.

Exercise15: 10 Negative Words You Use and Won't Use Again.

Change your negative words to positive phrases and capitalize them.

Negative	Positive
Can't	Will

Exercise 16: Write Down 5 Positive Words or Phrases to Say Out Loud Daily.

I remember when I was a child my mom had note cards on her bathroom mirror. They said things like, *I am more than a conqueror, I will have a good day, I will have a new house by December*, etc.

Determine your positive mantras and write them down, say them daily at least three times a day. This will change your life.

1.

2.

3.

4.

5.

Exercise 17: Write Your Mantras Down

Five positive mantras to repeat daily:

1.

2.

3.

4.

5.

Tanya Marchiol

NOTES

Tanya Marchiol

Tanya Marchiol

www.ingramcontent.com/pod-product-compliance
Lightning Source LLC
Chambersburg PA
CBHW070519200326
41519CB00013B/2854